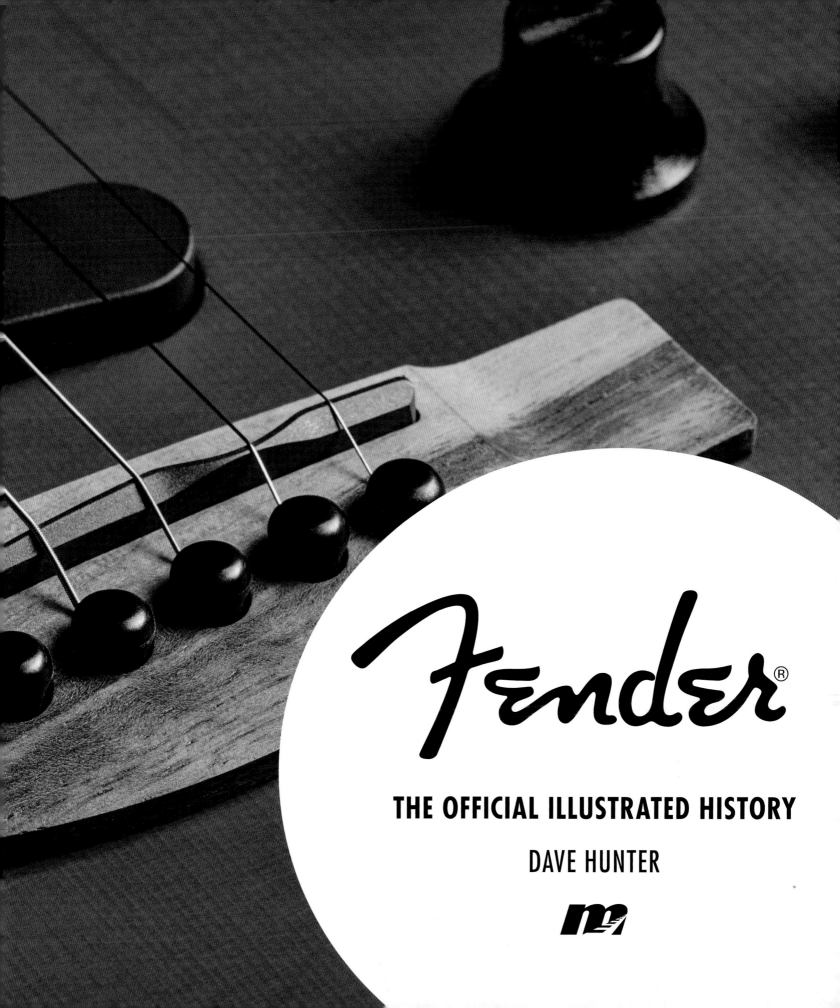

Fender®

THE OFFICIAL ILLUSTRATED HISTORY

DAVE HUNTER

Contents

Fender®

Introduction

If you uttered the phrase "electric guitar" any time in the past seven decades, chances are that nine out of ten people within earshot would immediately have pictured a Fender.

It's impossible to overstate the impact of Fender instruments, amplifiers, and effects upon the sound of popular music made over the past seventy-five years. Even so, we might begin to comprehend the weight of the company's influence by considering that, within less than a decade of its founding, Fender had delivered not one, not two, not three, but several instruments and amplifiers that were utterly groundbreaking and that set new standards of manufacture, playability, sound, and performance that remain benchmarks in the industry to this day.

In many ways, much of the popular music made over the past three quarters of a century simply *was* Fender music: the bright, twangy country guitar of the early 1950s or the gnarly, raw rock 'n' roll of the late 1950s; the wet-and-wild instrumental surf music of the early 1960s or the heavy, trippy psychedelic rock that took the stage a few years later; the powerful, bombastic arena rock of the 1970s; the lithe, wiry electric blues revival of the early 1980s or the grunge explosion at the end of that decade—all relied so heavily on the sound of Fender guitars, basses, and amplifiers that it's impossible to imagine these cultural waves having occurred without them.

From Jimmy Bryant and Bill Carson, to Dick Dale and Hank Marvin; from Buddy Holly and James Burton, to Jimi Hendrix and Ritchie Blackmore; from Keith Richards and Bruce Springsteen, to Stevie Ray Vaughan and Kurt Cobain, and on and on and on, the sound was Fender, and the impact was nothing short of revolutionary.

Looked at from the other side of the assembly line, Fender's impact on popular music—and, as a result, its impact on culture and society in the latter half of the twentieth century—was so significant because Leo Fender's vision was so greatly ahead of its time. The products of that vision defined the sound of rock 'n' roll before it even existed, then continued to evolve with the styles to provide musicians with exactly what they needed to sound fresh and exciting in genre after genre, from one era to the next.

Fender guitars and amplifiers earned respect so quickly because Leo made them, first and foremost, sound good and function well, able to survive the rigors of the road and to be easily serviceable. They weren't just supposed to look good in a department store window or catalog, or boast fancy semifunctional features, or appeal to passing trends that would find them gathering dust in attics and under beds once the next big thing hit the airwaves. They were utterly utilitarian and aimed entirely at professionals. Certainly, Leo and his company had to make a profit to stay in business, but they strove to make every new product the best it could be within a manufacturing budget that enabled them to still sell the things.

As a result, the company set new standards for quality and professionalism in the electric guitar and amplifier industries.

Because of this focus on quality, Fender creations represent some of the finest examples we have of culture and industry coming together to both define and fulfill a need. Leo Fender's knack for listening closely to musicians' expressions of those needs and adapting them to his work (rather than telling them what they *should* want) established practices that helped produce one guitar, amp, bass, and effects unit after another that quickly became a must-have among top artists of its day and beyond.

In 1946, the year Leo Fender founded his company, World War II was just barely behind us, gas cost fifteen cents per gallon, Perry Como held the highest position on the Billboard Top 100 with "Prisoner of Love," and as many as six thousand Americans were enjoying a new form of broadcast called television. As primitive as the era appears from the rearview mirror of the twenty-first century, within a few short years the Fender Musical Instrument Company developed electric instruments and amplifiers that are still among the most desired and relevant in the music world today, whether in original or reimagined form, and that remain in use by the most forward-looking artists of 2023 and beyond. A lot has happened in the past seventy-five years, but not once has a new musical style, trend, or craze ever threatened to make Fender's groundbreaking creations irrelevant.

CALIFORNIA DREAMIN'

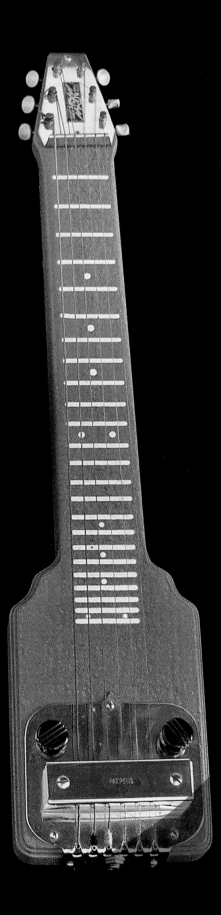

Young Leo Fender and the Radio Store

The story of Leo Fender's early life, up until the founding of the Fender Electric Instruments Company, appears, from our perspective in the twenty-first century, like a bridge between a very different and even ancient-seeming America to one on the cusp of modernity, just beginning to toddle toward the world we live in today. Any subject with such deep historical roots requires some examination of the era in which it was conceived in order to provide adequate context. The story of Fender's conception and founding of his revolutionary company fully makes sense only when considered alongside an exploration of the political, social, and cultural circumstances of the midcentury America into which it was born.

The world was in the midst of major flux at precisely the point Fender decided to launch a company to make electric instruments and amplifiers. Social norms, industry, cultural trends, and music would all be quite different—and they began careening rapidly toward *very* different—after World War II than they were before. In founding the company that bore his name in 1946, Fender was right at the demarcation point of that tectonic culture shift.

With its arc tied directly to dual revolutions in music and the musical instrument industry, the Fender company was primed to play an outsized part in influencing both. It would be inextricably intertwined with the tools for creating popular music and with how those tools were designed and manufactured, but as a result, also with how music *sounded*. It's all the more impressive that this profound influence came not from

one of the major guitar companies that were already active and thriving prior to the war—Gibson, Martin, Epiphone, Gretsch, Rickenbacker, or National—but from an upstart, a company barely established as an instrument manufacturer.

Ultimately the story of Fender's progress toward founding the world's most influential electric instrument company, and the stratospheric rise thereof, remains fascinating not only because of the unprecedented success that company would go on to experience; it's also the story of who we were as a nation and as a culture in the middle of the last century. As such, it also tells the tale of a time when that culture and a particular industry were conjoined, each influencing the other in roughly equal measure to drive the sound and feel of the music that would populate the soundtrack of our lives.

Before triggering that unquantifiable achievement, though, Fender had to find his path in an even more dramatically different, prewar America. And it wasn't always clear that that path would involve musical instruments.

MAIN:
K&F amplifier and lap-steel guitar, circa 1945.

RIGHT:
Detail of a record pressed at Fender's Radio Service.

A Fender is Born in Fullerton

Drive the stretch between Anaheim and Fullerton, California, today and you find yourself plying seemingly endless residential neighborhoods and business districts in what is largely considered the suburbs of southeast Los Angeles. Back in 1909, when Clarence Leonidas "Leo" Fender was born, however, the region was mostly rolling farmland, a parcel of which included the successful orange grove and farm run by his parents, Clarence Monte Fender and Harriet Elvira Wood. Born and raised on land not far from the later location of the first Fender factory, Leo had a relatively normal childhood for the times: school, work on the family farm, and a range of constructive hobbies, all of which combined to foment his groundbreaking endeavors a few decades later.

Leo attended the local public schools throughout his youth and showed a keen interest in radio and amplification electronics, and in all things mechanical, which served as his hobbies when he wasn't pitching in at the orange grove. His uncle, John West, ran an auto shop in Santa Maria. One year, he sent a box of salvaged electronics components to

Leo for Christmas, which helped fuel his desire to create something functional with this new technology. The following year, thirteen-year-old Leo visited his uncle's shop and was amazed by a creation he found there that had nothing to do with the auto repair that was West's stock-in-trade.

"He had built some radio equipment and had a large wooden trumpet speaker in front of his shop, pointed downtown to [amplify] radio programs," Fender recalled years later in a high school reunion speech. The clear, loud sound of that DIY radio clearly made an impact. "This acquainted me with radio," Leo added, "and led to my building amplifiers for musicians."[1]

While it's widely reported that Leo never learned to play the guitar, he did have a keen interest in music in general, played the saxophone in his high school band, and he had taken piano and trumpet lessons before that. He built an acoustic guitar at age sixteen and seems to have seen intuitively the potential link between musical instruments and electronic amplification from a relatively early age.

TOP LEFT: *A young Leo Fender (second from left) joins the family duck hunt.* TOP CENTER: *With orange trees in the background, a dapper Leo leans on the family car.* TOP RIGHT: *Though he never learned guitar, Leo played the saxophone, piano, and trumpet.* ABOVE: *A teenaged Leo in front of his school.*

From Accounting to Amplification

Upon graduating from Fullerton Union High School in 1928 (the same year the first AC vacuum tubes arrived on the market, as it happens, making amplifier design and construction much easier), Leo attended Fullerton Junior College, where he earned a two-year diploma in accounting.

Already an inveterate tinkerer, he built a PA system for a local band while working as a bookkeeper for the Consolidated Ice and Cold Storage Company in Anaheim in the early 1930s (having moved up the ladder from his first job there as a delivery man) and was soon building, renting out, and maintaining as many as half a dozen PA systems for musical performances, baseball games, fairs, and other events around Orange County and the environs surrounding Los Angeles. Already, it seems, the die was cast, even if Fender himself didn't quite know it yet.

In 1933, he met and fell in love with Esther Klosky, and the two married in 1934. Shortly thereafter, the newlyweds moved to San Luis Obispo, some 200 miles up the California coast, so Fender could take a job as an accountant with a tire company. The young bookkeeper hadn't considered leaving accounting for a career in music electronics until he lost what would be the last of his jobs in the field: the tire company, struggling as many were amid the Great Depression, cut its entire accounting department and left Fender unemployed.

This is perhaps the second of two twists of fate that saved Fender from an alternative future. The couple returned to Fullerton in 1938 and Leo took out a $600 loan with which to start his own business, a move that served as the springboard to the eventual creation of the company that would make him famous.

The first twist of fate had its seeds in a much earlier occurrence: at age eight, Feder had lost his left eye (accounts differ as to whether this was due to a tumor or a farm accident) and would forever after wear a glass eye in that socket. As he returned to Fullerton to open Fender's Radio Service with that $600 loan, World War II was just around the corner. Due to his visual impairment, however, he was among those young men deemed unfit to serve.

ABOVE: *Leo's first PA amplifier.* BELOW: *Leo mans his PA service at a civic event in Fullerton in the 1940s.*

FENDER RADIO SERVICE
112 S SPADRA
FULLERTON

PUBLIC ADDRESS SERVICE
FENDER RADIO
FULLERTON

Fender's Radio Service

More than just a place to get your radio repaired, Fender's shop was a full-service business, addressing the needs both of local music fans and musicians themselves. In addition to selling radios, records, and record players, Fender soon found himself repairing instruments and amplifiers brought in by local musicians who began asking him to build them new amps and PA systems.

From his first years in business, Fender displayed the propensity to listen to the needs of musicians and the knack for discerning flaws in existing designs—two traits that would greatly inform his later approaches to the design and construction of electric instruments and amplifiers, while also helping to distinguish his products in a crowded marketplace.

"Originally my work was design, modification, repair, and custom building," he said in 1971. "This gave me a wide acquaintance with competitive products and users' needs. Since my work encompassed more than musical equipment, I knew of benefits I could apply to the musicians' gear. I guess you would say the objectives were durability, performance, and tone."[2]

A genuine music enthusiast, if never a professional performer himself, Fender was known to have truly enjoyed the company of working musicians. He valued the raw and sometimes wacky ideas they would bring him, and also took constructive criticism of his creations as valuable means of evolving toward better and more suitable products.

Just as it did for any business dealing in components and commodities that were essential to the war effort, the United States' entry into World War II meant severe supply shortages for Fender's business and must have slowed his progress. Unlike many of the bigger guitar and amplifier manufacturers— some of which were forced to shut down entirely to serve the needs of the armed services—a small shop like Fender's could bob and weave and move a little more nimbly through the tough times, more often than not finding workarounds and acquiring necessary parts somewhere or other, and thus still serve the needs of local musicians.

Deep into the enforced austerity of the war years, Fender still managed to grow his notion of what his business should be, gradually moving away from the original retail model toward product development and manufacturing. "I liked developing new items that people needed. Working with tools and equipment was more to my liking than retail sales,"[3] he said in an interview in *Guitar Player* in 1971. It was clear that, even before the war was over, Fender had found a new direction for the business.

Records pressed at Fender's Radio Service, alongside an ad for the shop.

A New Partner and New Premises

Things were happening pretty quickly for Fender by the mid-1940s. Even while the business remained small and war shortages dictated certain limitations, his natural drive and application of critical thinking to the burgeoning need for better electric guitars and amplifiers were revealing a potential pioneer in the industry.

Fender had always valued the knowledge and skill of others working in the fledgling field, and around 1943 he saw an opportunity when he took on a partner. A local musician and inventor by the name of Clayton "Doc" Kauffman had been frequenting the shop for some time, and Fender was impressed with his designs for electric guitars and several unique pieces of hardware. Way back in 1929, Kauffman had designed a vibrato tailpiece that worked on both banjo and guitar, and for which he received a patent in 1932. He later designed a motorized vibrola unit that Rickenbacker used on guitars they released in 1937. He also designed and wound his own pickups.

In the early 1940s, Kauffman and Fender codesigned an automated record changer and sold the patent to another manufacturer for $5,000, which they used as seed money for the business. Around the same time, the pair also invented a pickup that had the instrument's strings pass through the coil windings. They filed a patent for that too, which was awarded in 1948 (patents often took several years to be granted at that time). Many reports also indicate that Kauffman and Fender built their first solidbody electric guitar as early as 1944, mainly as a testbed for their pickups. Demand for the instrument, however, found them renting it out to local musicians.

Meanwhile Fender and Kauffman were looking more and more like real manufacturers, turning out their own designs for electric Hawaiian (a.k.a. lap-steel) guitars and amplifiers. These were still extremely popular at the tail end of the Hawaiian music craze, which, in fact, segued neatly into the western swing craze, a genre in which the evocative slide-guitar sound loomed large.

South Harbor Boulevard in Fullerton, California.

ABOVE: *A crude lap steel made to test Fender and Kauffman's "boxcar" pickup.* RIGHT: *Label detail from a 1945 K&F amplifier, along with a rear view of the amp.* BELOW: *Hand-drawn design and advertisement for Fender and Kauffman's record changer.*

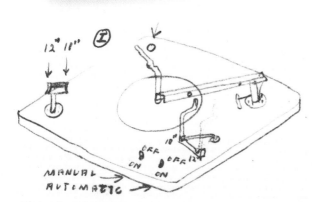

NOW ON DISPLAY
OUR NEW
Automatic Record Player

After servicing hundreds of automatic record players over a period of years we decided to build one as free as possible of faults.

The result is—an automatic mechanism having only one principle moving part (no multitude of springs, gears, and cams).

1. It plays 15 records automatically requiring approximately one second to change each record.
2. It has no bunch of tricky adjustments in the mechanism.
3. You cannot throw it out of adjustment by interfering with the action of the arm.
4. It is free from vibration through exclusive motor suspension principle.
5. It would require no costly cycle changes. 50 or 60 cycle current makes no difference to it.
6. It requires no spring mounting but will operate bolted solidly to the cabinet (an advantage in shipping). Other machines require delicate spring mounts to stay in questionable adjustment and to eliminate motor roar being amplified by the cabinet.
7. Fingertip adjustment will change the number of revolutions from 10 to 100 per minute.
8. There is nothing to jam, bind or bend as in other machines.
9. It has no wows or rumble, all notes are even and clear.
10. It won't chip or split records.
11. Due to few parts it is the strongest and lightest machine built.

Another Invention From
FENDER'S RADIO SHOP
MOST COMPLETELY EQUIPPED IN ORANGE COUNTY
107 South Spadra, Fullerton, Phone 6

Auto Radios — Records — Sheet Music
Electric Hawaiian and Standard Guitars

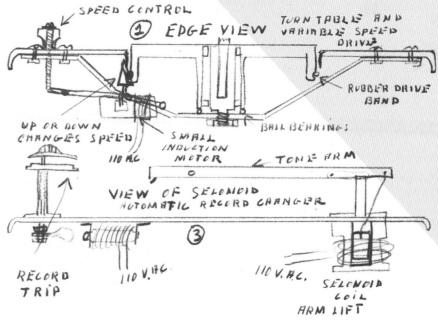

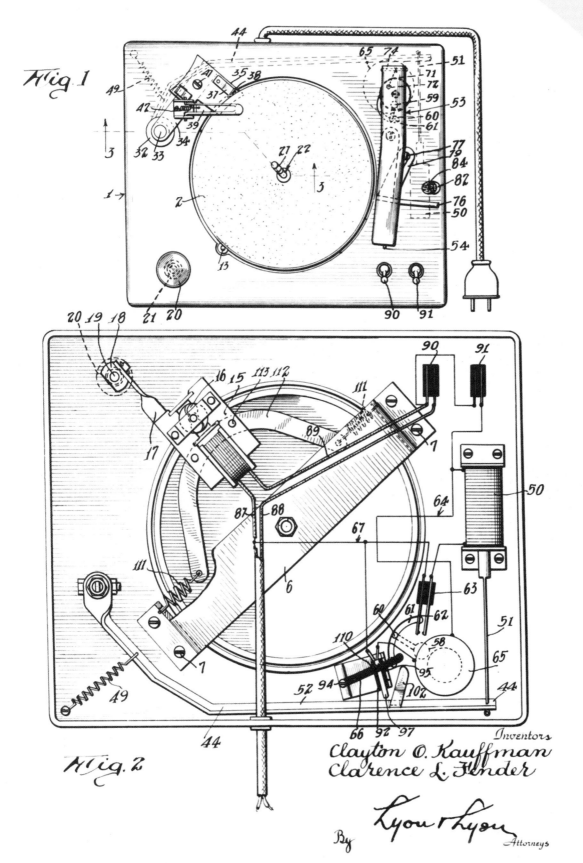

Fig. 1

Fig. 2

Inventors
Clayton O. Kauffman
Clarence L. Fender

By *Lyon & Lyon*
Attorneys

LEFT: *Diagrams on the patent application for the record changer.* OPPOSITE: *Leo at the punch press.*

In 1944 Fender's Radio Service acquired new, larger premises at 107 South Harbor Boulevard in Fullerton (formerly South Spadra). The following year, Kauffman and Fender made their existing partnership official by forming K&F Manufacturing Corp., which operated out of that address, with manufacturing spilling into a shack behind it when things got busy. The K&F logo appeared on several lap-steel guitars and amplifiers made and sold in that first year of the company's existence, but Kauffman quickly grew wary of the risks associated with owning a business. In February 1946 he traded his interest in K&F to Fender in exchange for a punch press, and the remaining partner lopped Kauffman's name from the company logo, forming Fender Electric Instruments shortly thereafter.

There was still plenty of hustling to be done, and more than a few bumps in the road lay ahead, but by now much of the groundwork was set for what would become the most influential company in the history of the electric guitar.

WOOD, WIRE & STEEL

The Birth of Fender Electric Instrument Co.

For many fans of Fender's groundbreaking creations, the company's history begins in 1950 with the introduction of the world's first successful production-model solidbody electric guitar. This was the culmination of four years—beginning with the company's founding in 1946—packed with developments and innovations that charted a direct path to the solidbody's revolutionary release. The work leading up to that moment helped define the Fender sound, even if in somewhat different forms.

In its short year of existence, the K&F Manufacturing Corp. run by Doc Kauffman and Leo Fender produced six models of lap-steel (Hawaiian) electric guitars and three amplifiers. The lap-steels and amplifiers were paired according to their size and features in sets aimed at students, novices, and professionals respectively. Hitting the ground running in 1946, Leo and the four employees he retained from K&F carried on in much the same way, although it's generally acknowledged that production quality increased fairly quickly as Leo devoted his attention more fully to the effort.

With the shift to the new company, Fender also began to partner with a new distributor. For several years, Leo had purchased electronic components from the Radio & Television Equipment Co. (Radio-Tel) in Santa Ana—more specifically from Don Randall, the salesman for the Fullerton area, who also served as Radio-Tel's general manager. While encouraging Fender to ramp up his own manufacturing, Randall also convinced the owner of Radio-Tel, F. C. Hall, that they should distribute products made by Fender Electric Instrument Co. Before the end of Fender company's first year in business, a deal was penned to do just that.

MAIN:
Fender lap-steel guitars and accompanying "woody" amplifiers.

RIGHT:
The 1950 catalog cover featured a three-neck lap-steel.

FAR RIGHT:
Don Randall, the general manager of Radio-Tel, convinced Leo to ramp up production in 1946. He also convinced his boss, F. C. Hall, that Radio-Tel should become Fender's distributor.

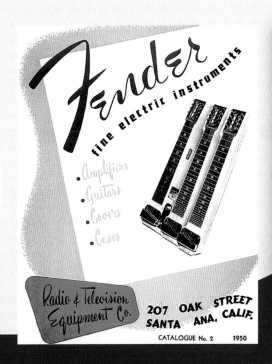

Upgrading the Amplifiers

Early in 1946 Leo introduced a new lineup of Fender amplifiers and single-neck lap-steel guitars, paired from more affordable to more expensive models: the Princeton, Deluxe, and Professional. All but the smaller Princeton amplifier wore the new lightning bolt Fender logo. Fender amps from this era have probably remained the most distinguished among early Fender products. Nicknamed "woodies," each came in a lustrously finished hardwood cabinet—available in maple, black walnut, mahogany, and, occasionally, oak—three shiny protective metal grille strips, and a fixed wooden handle on top, representing a major upgrade in both style and construction from the K&F amplifiers of just a few months before.

Although there would be some notable developments in the electric Hawaiian guitar line, it's widely acknowledged that Fender's amplifier development was coming along by leaps and bounds. Just a year after introducing the appealing woodies, Fender—still a tiny company by any standard—unveiled what many vintage amp authorities today consider one of the most significant evolutionary leaps ever in amp design: the Dual Professional.

In addition to bringing an enduring new look to the Fender lineup with its cabinet covered in aircraft-grade linen—a variation of the tweed covering that would adorn Fender amps until 1960—the Dual Professional introduced several major innovations:

- The world's first production amplifier to carry two speakers (a pair of 10-inch Jensens)
- The first Fender (and one of the first-ever guitar amps) to carry a top-mounted chassis with upward-facing control panel
- The first Fender with a removable back panel for easy circuitry access
- One of the first production guitar amps to have its electronic components mounted to a circuit board
- The first Fender amp with a tube chart
- The first Fender amp made with a finger-jointed pine cabinet[4]

The Dual Professional was also distinguished by its wedge-shaped (a.k.a. V-front) cabinet, designed to increase the dispersion of the two speakers. This feature was retained the following year when the model name was changed to the Super. All single-speaker Fender amplifiers were eventually migrated to tweed-covered cabinets that have come to be known as TV fronts for their resemblance to early television sets.

OPPOSITE TOP: *Billy F Gibbons with a brace of Esquires and a stack of V-front amplifiers.*
OPPOSITE BOTTOM: *1949 V-front Super. Introduced in 1947 as the Dual Professional, the amps featured a wedge design to disperse sound.* **ABOVE:** *George Fullerton's brother Bob shows off a pair of TV-front amps outside the early Fullerton facilities.* **RIGHT:** *A 1951 TV-front Princeton amplifier. Fender single-speaker amps migrated to this tweed-covered design.*

The Birth of the Twang

Early Fender lap-steel guitars used strings-through pickups (nicknamed "boxcar" pickups) that Fender and Kauffman had developed for K&F's electric Hawaiian guitars. These were bright, clear-sounding pickups, but they didn't quite have the tone most closely associated with Fender guitars to come. In 1948, however, Fender introduced an amp-and-lap-steel set that was another rung down the ladder from the Princeton, toward the student end of the spectrum. The Champion, later shortened to Champ, is perhaps best remembered for the diminutive amp model that became a perennial favorite with beginners and studio pros alike. At the same time, the electric Hawaiian guitar that accompanied the Champ ushered in a new style of pickup that would set the standard for the majority of future essential Fender tone components.

The pickup on the six-string Champion lap-steel was made from pressed-fiber top and bottom plates through which six holes were drilled to hold six Alnico rod magnets; several turns of wire were wound around these to form a coil. This is how all noteworthy Fender pickups in the future would be made: other than seeing baseplates with a slightly different shape, most Fender fans today would take one look at a late-1940s Champ pickup and say, "Hey, a Telecaster pickup!" (In fact, the near-interchangeability of the two has led many contemporary players to pull the pickups from relatively affordable early Champ lap-steels, add an appropriate baseplate, and mount them into their latter-day Telecasters to achieve vintage-certified tone.)

With this new pickup design, even before the development of his ground-breaking solidbody guitar, Fender was establishing the bright, cutting, yet muscular and twangy tone that would become the Fender sonic signature. In the early days of the amplified guitar, so much of the instrument's development was about cutting through the muddy mix of a live band. To that end, brightness and clarity were often the goal. Early success in achieving this—and firmly establishing "that sound" even before going to market with an electric Spanish guitar—was crucial to Fender's eventual broader success.

"I think that perhaps I was the first person to use separate magnets, one for each string," Leo told *Guitar Player* in May 1978. "That way, I found that the notes didn't seem to run together—you could get more of an individual performance off of each string."[5] In addition to the individual magnets, the narrow coil and tight magnetic field contributed to a bright tone, another boon to the guitarist's effort to "cut through the band."

Riding a Rough Road

By the summer of 1947 Fender had added to its manufacturing facilities by constructing a pair of simple metal sheds on Santa Fe Avenue, near the corner of Pomona Avenue, and the team had grown to around six employees. Despite several promising early developments in amplifiers and electric Hawaiian guitars, the young company often struggled to survive in its early years. Leo was putting everything he had into keeping the company afloat, often doing whatever he could on the side to keep ahead of the bank loans.

The company's team was already coming together. One longtime Fender team member, a former car salesman named Dale Hyatt, had already joined the company in 1946. Hyatt transitioned from being a foreman of sorts to overseeing the remaining Fender Radio Shop and eventually playing a major role in sales.

George Fullerton, an electronics enthusiast and part-time musician, was already familiar with Fender's business, having occasionally taken over his PA-for-hire duties before becoming an employee early in 1948. Born in 1923 in Hindsville, Arkansas (and unrelated to Fullerton, California), Fullerton moved to California before the war to work in a plant manufacturing aircraft parts.

By this time, too, three women were working on assembly in Fender's manufacturing facility. Occasional help was also provided by an electronics whiz named Ray Massey.

In an interview with author Tony Bacon in the early 1990s, Fullerton described Leo's entrepreneurial sidelines in the mid-1940s:

When I really got acquainted with Leo, there used to be a park in Fullerton on the west side of town called Amerige Park. They would have community happenings. They always had some kind of celebration on the 4th of July, and—I believe it was '47—Leo used to supply the amplifier and sound system for these programs.

Leo had a panel truck, flat-top and long bodied, and he'd mount speakers on top of it, play music. When they had community happenings he would have somebody drive this van up and down the street advertising the event. There were other occasions that he used these speakers, one was the Sunrise Service on Easter Sunday that used to take place on top of Hillcrest Park.[6]

While scrambling to make it all work and continually striving to improve product, Fender bounced over plenty of bumps in the road. Forrest White first met Leo in 1948 and would join the Fender company in 1954, eventually rising to vice president. In 1994 White published a memoir entitled *Fender: The Inside Story*, where he recounted many of Leo's tales about the early years. White reported Fender once telling him: "Those early years were absolute hell. I think I worked from six in the morning 'til midnight every day of the week. A new trademark is a hard thing to get accepted. With no advertising, no one knew who we were and there was nothing to pep up sales. It took every penny I could get my hands on to keep things together. I was unhappy with our distributor [F. C. Hall and Radio-Tel], who was a former shipping clerk and never advertised."[7]

Beyond lacking sales resulting from what Leo saw as Radio-Tel's underwhelming performance, there was also the occasional genuine hardship, which must have been a significant blow to any young company struggling to stay afloat. Of one such incident in 1947, Fender told White: "[Radio-Tel] didn't sell hardly any of our [Hawaiian] guitars. They just sat there in this garage, and termites got into them and ate through the bodies. We never found out about the termites until dealers started calling us about holes in the guitars. We ended up taking back 500 guitars and had to burn them all. On top of that, I was being sued by four people simultaneously, and I had to get an extra building because there wasn't enough space left in the radio shop."[8]

White speculated that termites are unlikely to have gotten into finished lap-steel bodies; chances are the wood already contained termites. Either way, it's easy to imagine the impact that reclaiming and destroying five hundred instruments must have had on the young operation.

OPPOSITE LEFT: *1952 Champ model lap-steel. The Champ's pickup would set the template for all noteworthy future Fender pickups.* OPPOSITE RIGHT: *A better look at the pickup in a 1949 model.* LEFT: *By 1947 Fender had constructed two simple metal sheds on Santa Fe Avenue, near the corner of Pomona Avenue.*

Powering Through and Prototyping the Future

Not that there weren't successes. Along with the Dual Professional amplifier of 1947, Fender introduced an impressive double-neck electric Hawaiian guitar called the Dual 8 Professional (for its eight strings on each neck). Later that year, Fender even introduced some early triple-neck guitars, the model name for which would solidify as the Custom Triple (popularly, the 3-Neck) by 1948 or 1949.

In addition to notable product developments, Fender was getting enough name recognition and achieving enough endorsements from several artists on the busy Los Angeles music scene to indicate promise in the fledgling endeavor—and to encourage further effort. Some of those names might be forgotten in popular music circles today, but many were significant artists on the western swing scene of the day, and they helped spread the Fender brand even before it landed on a solidbody electric Spanish guitar.

Noel Boggs, an early star of the steel guitar who played with Spade Cooley and Bob Wills, played a Fender electric Hawaiian (sometimes called a console steel when mounted on legs, as they often were) and Professional amp almost right from their introduction in 1946. Another former Bob Wills sideman, Leon McCauliffe, was one of the most highly regarded steelers of his day, so his move from a Rickenbacker double-neck to a Fender Dual Professional lap-steel in 1947 marked a big coup for Leo and company. McCauliffe later moved up to a Fender triple-neck, and even a monster quad-neck console steel in later years.

Hank Williams' steel player, Don Helms, also took up Fender's Dual Professional steel and a Pro amp to go with it, while Herb Remington, another star steel player with the Texas Playboys, once spoke about having tuning problems with his Rickenbacker double-neck, "until Fender got me on one of his guitars."[9]

Hank Williams's steel player, Don Helms (far left), took up Fender's Dual Professional steel.

And while most early Fender players were, unsurprisingly, steel guitarists working out of the LA area, it's interesting to note that the Fender name was already making its way across the country. Bob Foster, playing with Cowboy Copas (for whom Hank Garland also played guitar), played both a Fender steel guitar and Professional amplifier as far away as Nashville and on tour in the Midwest and eastern states.

Fender's reputation for tone and quality was solidifying on the western swing scene. Leo and company were also starting to prototype an instrument that, though initially laughed at by steel-guitar players of the day, would nevertheless revolutionize the industry just a year and a half later.

LEFT: *Noel Boggs, an early star of the steel guitar, is seen with his famous Leo-built four-neck Stringmaster.* ABOVE: *Former Bob Wills sideman Leon McCauliffe moved from a Rickenbacker double-neck to a Fender Dual Professional lap-steel in 1947, and even a monster Fender quad-neck console steel in later years.* TOP: *Instrumental duo Santo & Johnny sported a Fender three-neck lap-steel on the cover of their eponymous 1959 LP.*

Women at Fender and a Growing Company

Collectors and players fortunate enough to have owned Fender guitars or amplifiers made in the early days of the company have often observed that several women played a significant role in manufacturing their prized piece. Penciled initials inside guitar and lap-steel body cavities provide clues to the workers who helped to craft the instruments, but amplifiers in particular have revealed many of the hands that wired, soldered, and assembled them, thanks to first names signed on short strips of masking tape cut with pinking shears and stuck inside the lower wall of the chassis. More often than not, these have pointed to the women who played an important role in the fledgling factory right from the start.

One of these workers, Maybelle "Vangie" Ortega, was said to be the second or third employee hired at Fender (other than Leo himself). In the late 1940s, she helped bring her sister, Irene Vasquez, into the fold.

Responding to questions about the early days via her grandson, Matthew Logan Vasquez, Irene reported, "Leo was the nicest guy you could hope to meet and was like a father to me. He was always very organized. I would wire amps and guitars, and he always had everything color coordinated for us to put them together easier."

"The first factory was composed of corrugated metal and chain-link," she also recalled. "It was somewhat exposed to the elements. You had to walk across the street to the gas station if you wanted to use the restroom."

On his grandmother's behalf, Logan Vasquez further reported, "She was always very proud to have worked for Fender and only said good things about him."

Even as it struggled to survive as a business in the late 1940s, Fender looked like a real company—all the more so, in hindsight, given the major breakthrough that was just around the corner. A photograph taken in 1949 shows most of the company's employees gathered outside one of the sheet-metal buildings that comprised the Fender factory. We can see Bob Fullerton, Fred Fullerton, George Fullerton, Don Kroener, Lyle Burke, Louis Lugar, Cecil Shawbell, Lawrence Norberg, Lupe Lopez, Lydia Sanchez, Vangie Ortega, and an unidentified man, with others—Irene Vasquez included—believed to have been in the workforce but absent from the frame.[10] The twelve personnel shown don't include Leo himself (a camera buff who might have taken the photo), Dale Hyatt (who was manning Fender Radio Service until its closure in 1951), or a handful of others who freelanced with Fender now and then. In other words, this was the core team that would soon revolutionize the guitar industry.

Irene Vasquez (left) and a colleague cover a Fender lap-steel in acetate.

"Queen of Tone" Abby Ybarra winds pickups in 1959 and later inside the Fender Custom Shop. She retired in 2013 after 57 years.

TWANG COMES TO TOWN

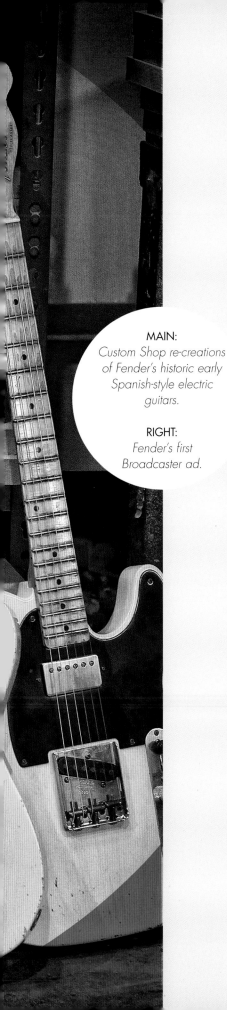

The Telecaster Arrives

By the late 1940s notable makers such as Gibson, Gretsch, and Epiphone had offered successful electric Spanish guitars for more than a decade. But these big, fully hollow-bodied archtops were rife with problems for many professional players: the warm tone worked well in solo jazz performances, but often these instruments couldn't deliver the bite and brightness that western swing players, in particular, needed to compete with the lap-steel guitar; such guitars weren't possessed of great sustain; and the big hollowbodies were prone to howling feedback once the amp was turned up loud enough to be heard amid a raging band.

MAIN:
Custom Shop re-creations of Fender's historic early Spanish-style electric guitars.

RIGHT:
Fender's first Broadcaster ad.

Many in the industry were beginning to see the solidbody electric as a viable product rather than a novelty or test bed for components. So far, though, no one had grasped the nettle, and the young and still relatively small Fender company found itself strangely well positioned to be first to get this new and seemingly far-fetched notion off the drawing board and out the door.

It wasn't an entirely new idea. Bigsby and Rickenbacker had both produced solid electric Spanish guitars: the former in very limited numbers on a bespoke basis, and the latter without any consistency. The way that Fender would attack the solidbody electric guitar embraced a new and comprehensive rethink of the entire concept.

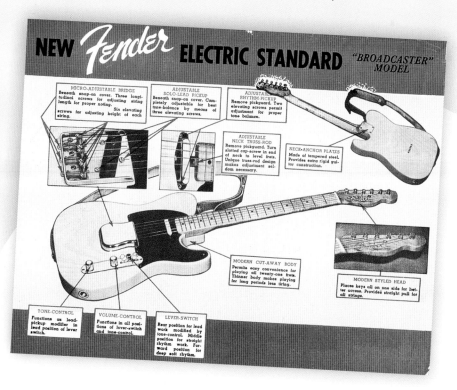

Prototyping a Revolution

The company continued to manufacture its bread-and-butter lap-steel guitars and accompanying amplifiers in the final year of the formative 1940s, but Fender also spent much of its energies in 1949 working toward designing a viable solidbody electric Spanish guitar. In a sense, the small outfit from Fullerton already had a head start over bigger guitar makers that had previously released hollowbody electric Spanish guitars: Fender had only ever made production solidbody lap-steel guitars, and their bright, clear, sustaining sound had been praised by players on the western swing scene for a few years already, becoming a standard tone for electric guitarists in that genre. In this sense, Fender already had the desired sound in its arsenal—it just needed to convert the electric Hawaiian template to the electric Spanish format.

Looking back on his efforts three decades later, Fender told *Guitar Player*, "I guess you would say the objectives were durability, performance, and tone."[11] Following from this, as he told *Rolling Stone* in 1976, "The design of everything we did was intended to be easy to build, and easy to repair. . . . If a thing is easy to service, it is easy to build."[12] The two statements amount to the foundational principles for Fender's approach to electric guitars. The utilitarian nature of Fender instruments had already been proven in their lap-steel guitars; now these principles would be applied to an entirely new blueprint for the electric Spanish guitar, resulting in an instrument the likes of which the world had never seen.

Leo Fender himself would take the lead on the design of the electronics and hardware for the new model. We've already seen how the bridge pickup for the electric Spanish guitar evolved from the unit used in Champion lap-steels, with individual pole piece magnets for clarity, brightness, and articulation. The neck pickup would be a twist on the same idea: a smaller and slightly lower-powered unit with a nickel-plated cover to dress up its spotlight position near the end of the fingerboard. The otherwise exposed poles and black top plate of the bridge pickup were intended to be hidden by the "ashtray" bridge cover with which the production guitars were eventually shipped.

In addition to their pickups, the sound and functionality of the guitars that would arrive as the Broadcaster, Esquire, and Telecaster were largely defined by the new and original bridge that Leo designed for them. Even before the guitars were released to the public, Fender sought to protect his design with a patent application filed on January 13, 1950 (granted a little over a year later), for a "Combination Bridge and Pickup Assembly." Drawings included with the application clearly show the very recognizable Tele bridge plate with three saddles and a pickup suspended beneath (all mounted on an extremely rudimentary guitar that lacks even a cutaway and carries a three-per-side headstock). As iconic as the Telecaster body shape has become, this mating of hardware and electronics in one simple and ingeniously functional design really is what defines the model, particularly the iconic twangy-yet-meaty sound of its bridge pickup.

After taking up with the young Fender company full-time in 1948, George Fullerton began assuming a bigger role in product development, eventually becoming Leo's right-hand man in several capacities. Fullerton, who had displayed an interest in art and design that complemented his technical abilities, was tasked with designing the new guitar's body. The eventual results, a simple yet elegant outline for a solid-wood guitar with single cutaway, stands alongside the best examples of midcentury modern design and remains current after more than seventy years.

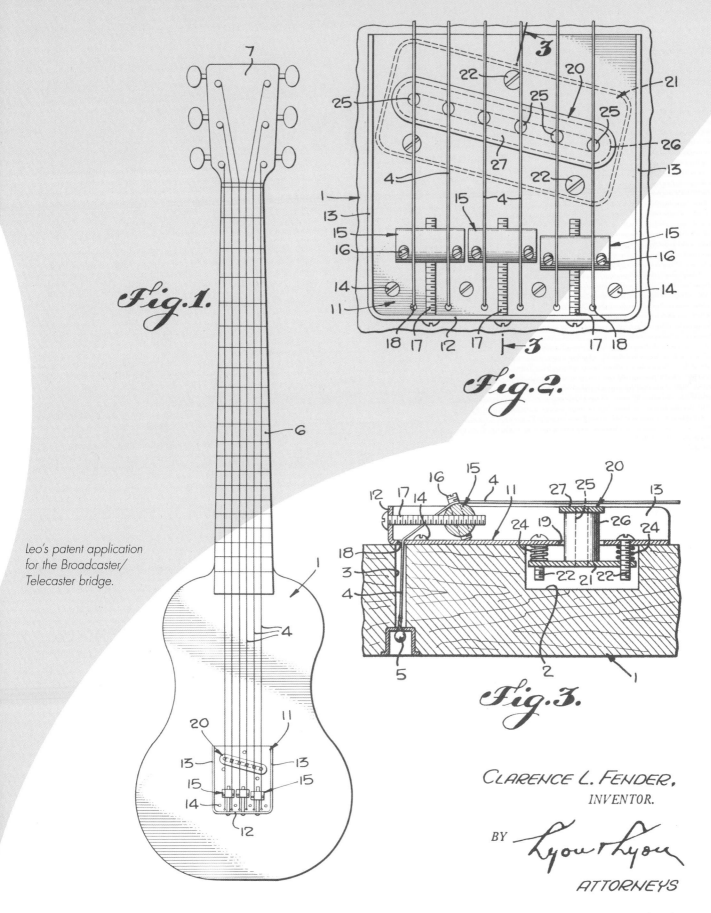

Leo's patent application for the Broadcaster/Telecaster bridge.

Fig.1.

Fig.2.

Fig.3.

CLARENCE L. FENDER,
INVENTOR.

BY

ATTORNEYS

A Guitar Is Born

The first fully conceived prototype of the new model was in hand at Fender partway through 1949, and it clearly wore the distinctive body shape, hardware, and electronics that would become signatures of the guitar most famous as the Telecaster. Several telltale signs differentiate this prototype from the standard model—the three-per-side tuners on the snakehead headstock, a smaller, more generic-looking pickguard, the shorter and somewhat angled control plate—but it's a clear signpost for the direction Fender was going.

Less obvious at first glance was the pine body beneath the opaque white finish, and the neck (as hinted at by the lack of a skunk stripe at the back) lacked a truss rod, while also being screwed onto the body through a slightly longer 2⅝-inch plate. Another crucial element of the design was the 25½-inch scale length, something that would become a standard for Fender's most popular electric guitars. As it turns out, this dimension was selected somewhat by chance.

"Leo told me the scale and fret placement had been copied from a Gretsch archtop guitar," Forrest White recalled. "This is why it was 25½ inches from the nut to the bridge."[13] Many other popular guitars of the day, several Gibsons included, used a slightly shorter 24¾-inch scale length, but the 25½-inch scale—which would follow on the Stratocaster and Jazzmaster—enhanced the bright, shimmering response that Fender was chasing, while helping to retain a bold, tight low end on the wound strings, both of which have become archetypes of the Fender sound.

Fender produced other prototypes through the rest of 1949 and into early 1950 as the model approached its now-legendary form, but there were still a few big bumps in the road before it became the classic design we know today. "I took the original guitar—at first

we called it the Esquire, looked just like the Telecaster—to the trade show in Chicago," Don Randall told Tony Bacon in 1992; in 1949 Randall was still with Fender's distributor, Radio-Tel. "I just got laughed out of the place. It was called everything from a canoe paddle to the snow shovel."[14]

Of more practical concern, though, the preproduction Esquire's exposure to the light of day revealed potential design flaws—and, for all his genius, Leo Fender wasn't always receptive to outside critiques of his work (other than, it would seem, from the musicians who earned their pay with his creations).

Of his first outing with the Esquire, Randall further recalled:

> A guy from National/Valco, Al Frost, he came and looked at it. And he said, "Don, do you have a neck [truss] rod in it?" I said, "No, it's just a solid maple neck—we don't need one." He said, "Look, I want to tell you one thing. If you don't have a neck rod in it, you're in for a lot of trouble. We've been through this and I can tell you first hand."
>
> So I contacted Leo, I says, "Leo, we've got to have a neck rod in there." "No," [said Leo], "we don't need one, it's rock maple." I said, "I tell you one thing, either we put a neck rod in that, or we don't sell it! Now make up your mind to it!"[15]

As Randall indicated, several preproduction examples of the new guitar were given the name "Esquire," but by the guitar's official release partway through 1950, the flagship two-pickup model had been dubbed the Broadcaster, while the more affordable single-pickup model was called the Esquire. This was not the last name change imposed on Fender's new electric guitar, but the form had been cast, and it would prove a revolution in the making.

OPPOSITE: *Fender employees complete and test Broadcasters. Note the metal factory walls.* **ABOVE:** *A circa 1949 snakehead prototype of Fender's first solidbody Spanish-style electric guitar.*

A Fender Solidbody Hits the Streets

Widely differing tales from those who were there at the time—and the sad fact that none of them are with us today to confirm an accurate account—mean that the real stories of which version of Fender's early solidbody hit the street first, how many were produced, and precisely when they came to market are difficult to discern seventy years on.

Some existing reports from trade magazines of the day indicate that only the single-pickup Esquire was displayed at the summer 1950 National Association of Music Merchants (NAMM) show in Chicago. It's also known that Don Randall and Radio-Tel urged the release of a more affordable, single-pickup guitar first, considering it an easier sell. Running contrary to that, however, Forrest White later reported that Leo

Fender and Don Randall both told him that the dual-pickup model was ready for the 1950 summer NAMM show: "The guitar that made the show that year was a two-pickup version with truss rod. Leo and Don called it the Broadcaster."[16] That said, White didn't work at Fender until 1954, so we may need to take this report with a grain of salt.

Meanwhile Esquires with two pickups and the more familiar blond finishes were also made early in 1950, as evidenced by photographs and existing examples; one taken by Leo himself shows just such a two-pickup Esquire in blond finish, with the absence of a walnut teardrop on the headstock behind the nut, indicating it lacked a truss rod. To further confuse matters, Leo told *Guitar Player* in 1984, "[Don]

Randall wanted us to come out with the single-pickup design and wanted to call it the Esquire. That may be why it showed up in that catalogue and price list and the Broadcaster or Telecaster didn't. But the Broadcaster was the first one we built."[17]

Whatever the case, Fender's debut solidbody electric Spanish guitar was firmly on the map by mid- to late 1950, and, if it wasn't entirely an overnight success, it certainly sent major ripples through the industry before year's end. Pricing for the single-pickup Esquire at the time of its NAMM debut in July 1950 ran $139.95 for the guitar and $39.95 for the case. By the following fall, the two-pickup Broadcaster was listed in the sales catalog at $169.95 plus $39.95 for the case.

THIS PAGE: *A photograph of Broadcaster #0075 made by Leo himself, alongside a re-creation by John Peden using the same guitar and case.* OPPOSITE TOP: *A rare original 1950 Broadcaster, serial number 0005.* OPPOSITE BOTTOM: *Bill of materials for manufacture and finishing of a Broadcaster body.*

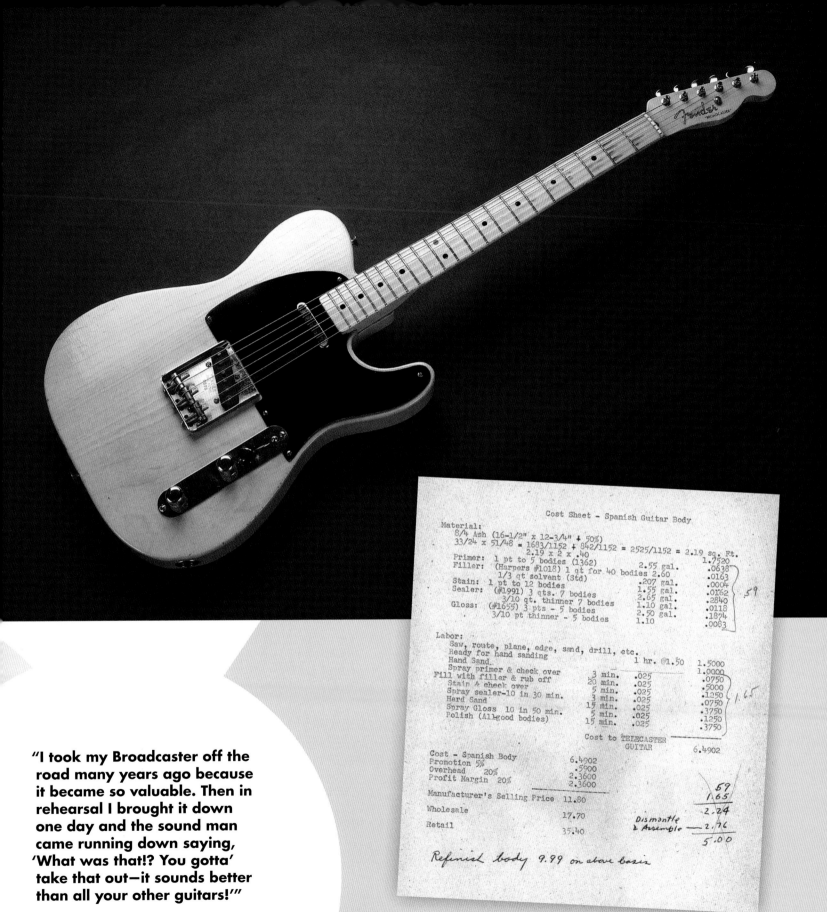

"I took my Broadcaster off the road many years ago because it became so valuable. Then in rehearsal I brought it down one day and the sound man came running down saying, 'What was that!? You gotta' take that out—it sounds better than all your other guitars!'"

MIKE CAMPBELL
Interview with Dave Hunter,
April 1999

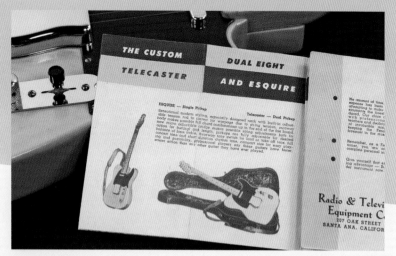

ABOVE: *The Broadcaster/Telecaster neck pickup and hang tag.*
OPPOSITE: *Fender employee Hugh Garriott demonstrates the strength of a Broadcaster neck.*

And, no surprise: as much as the humble and seemingly omnipresent Telecaster is taken for granted today, at the time of its release it represented a total reimagining of the guitar in general, a genius-level piece of design that stripped down and entirely reconceived how the instrument should look, feel, and sound, as well as how it could be constructed. Perhaps the greatest mark of Fender's design success is the fact that so many major artists today continue to turn to Telecasters— guitars that are very little changed from the first production Broadcasters—as their cherished number ones.

It's entirely understandable that such a radical instrument might take a little time to generate a comprehensive uptake, but its benefits were clear to several players from the start, and Leo Fender's unwavering grasp of their design goals—and the unprecedented boon to players that resulted—helped keep the effort firmly on-message. As the lists of original features in early ads humbly indicated, these guitars clearly delivered more advances in guitar design and construction than any single new instrument in the history of the Spanish-style guitar. An insert to the Radio-Tel sales catalog entitled "New Fender Electric Standard— 'Broadcaster Model'" boasted of several of these:

- Micro-adjustable Bridge
- Adjustable Solo-Lead Pickup
- Adjustable Rhythm Pickup
- Adjustable Neck Truss Rod
- Neck Anchor Plates
- Tone Control
- Volume Control
- Lever Switch
- Modern Cutaway
- Modern Styled Head

A short time later, a trade magazine advertisement added a few other essential features to the list:

- Fine fast action
- True intonation
- No feedback
- Last fret position accessible

If we take many of these features for granted today, we have Fender—and the Telecaster, specifically—to thank for bringing them to the game in the first place

Players Gonna Play

With a solid new guitar under his belt, Leo Fender was eager to test the waters. If it would take several months for the wider playing world to get a feel for the new solidbody, some of the scene's hottest pickers were quicker on the uptake.

In 1984 Leo told *Guitar Player* about the time he took an early Broadcaster to the Riverside Rancho Dance Hall in Riverside, California, for Jimmy Bryant to try out. Bryant took the guitar up on stage with Little Jimmy Dickens and his band and started playing, and, as Fender recalled, "Pretty soon the band stopped, everybody on the dance floor stopped, and they all gathered around Jimmy when he played."[18]

Bryant would adopt the Broadcaster as his main squeeze, using it to fire off blistering, virtuosic speed-picking runs alongside equally fleet-fingered steel player Speedy West, making Bryant the first major ambassador of Fender's new electric-Spanish guitar.

"Jimmy played things on guitar that nobody else could play," George Fullerton would later recall. "And, of course, this was an electric guitar with low action—and with that cutaway, he could go right up the neck. So naturally we put one in his hand, and this was like starting a prairie fire. Pretty soon we couldn't make enough of those guitars. . . . Jimmy was on television shows, personal appearances, and everybody wanted a guitar like Jimmy Bryant's."[19]

Several other significant players on the western swing scene, many of whom were already playing Fender amplifiers, grabbed their own Esquires and Broadcasters, often before the model was officially in production. Spade Cooley guitarist Jimmy Wyble, who played alongside Fender steel player Noel Boggs, was pictured with a black Esquire as early as May 1950 and was also photographed playing a blond model around the same time. Soon Bill Carson, also with Spade Cooley, as well as taking sideman duties with Hank Thompson and Wade Ray, was playing the new Fender electric, too, and vying for a job as a test pilot for Leo in a deal that would help him purchase his own new Telecaster and amplifier.

"I believe Jimmy Bryant, Buck Owens, Jimmy Page, Muddy Waters . . . were all on to something. Just listen to any of these folks' recordings and you'll agree: the sound is exhilarating, exciting, and just cuts through the mix in an awesome way."

REDD VOLKAERT Interview with Dave Hunter, May 2012

OPPOSITE: *Doc Kaufman plays a Broadcaster through a V-front Super at the Fender factory.* **TOP:** *Guitar virtuoso Jimmy Bryant and a Nocaster in an early ad.* **LEFT:** *A rare color shot of legendary guitar-and-steel team of Jimmy Bryant and Speedy West in El Monte, California.*

As the 1950s rolled on, the Broadcaster (and its descendants) became synonymous with the twangy tone central to the electric guitar sound in country music, but across the same decade it would also proliferate to all genres of popular music.

From the rock 'n' roll of Paul Burlison and James Burton, to the blues of Muddy Waters and Albert Collins, to the arena rock of Keith Richards, Jimmy Page, and Bruce Springsteen, and the punk of Joe Strummer and D. Boon, the Telecaster has established an unshakable position at the center of popular music. The Telecaster has also abetted the chops of some of the guitar's most accomplished virtuosi, Danny Gatton, Roy Buchanan, Albert Lee, Jim Campilongo, Brent Mason, Brad Paisley, and John 5 among them. That the Fender Telecaster continues to be one of the most played and revered instruments in the hands of groundbreaking guitarists today, often in forms that have changed very little from the Broadcasters that rolled off the line in late 1950, is perhaps the most incontrovertible evidence of the genius of the original design brought forth by Leo and his team more than seventy years ago.

RIGHT: *Paul Burlison (seated) with Johnny and Dorsey Burnette of the Rock and Roll Trio.* **OPPOSITE BOTTOM LEFT:** *Art Smith in an early Fender ad.* **OPPOSITE TOP AND CENTER:** *The February 20 telegram from Gretsch asking Fender to discontinue using the Broadcaster name, and the February 21 letter from Don Randall to Fender salesmen announcing the discontinuation of the model name.*

RADIO & TELEVISION EQUIPMENT CO.

WHOLESALE MUSIC DIVISION
207 OAK STREET   SANTA ANA CALIFORNIA   KIMBERLY 2-6741

February 21, 1951

TO ALL SALESMEN:

From this date forward you will not refer to our Dual
pickup Spanish guitar as the Broadcaster guitar. We
have been advised that this is an infringement on a
copyrighted name of another manufacturer and they have
requested that we abandon the name immediately. We
have checked this and are inclined to agree that they
are fair in their request. Consequently, it behooves
us to find a new name. As soon as a new name is found
you will be advised and in the meantime, please advise
all your customers that the Broadcaster name will be
changed.

It is a shame that our efforts in both selling and
advertising are lost but I am sure we can change over
with little if any detrimental effects. If any of you
have a good name in mind I would welcome hearing from
you immediately.

                    Yours very truly,

                    RADIO & TELEVISION EQUIPMENT CO.

                    Donald D. Randall
                    General Manager

DDR: cp

Who is making the complaint? put out a bulleton to the dealers making a contest, offering a guitar for the best name.

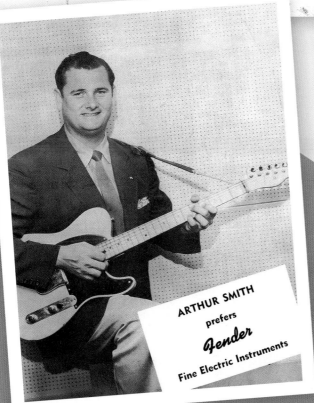

ARTHUR SMITH
prefers
Fender
Fine Electric Instruments

Name-Dropping

As iconic and utterly *right* as the seminal design was, it would occasionally be altered and upgraded over the years to come, sometimes very subtly, other times more dramatically. One early alteration arrived in a simple change of name: in February 1951, just as the Broadcaster was beginning to gain a little acceptance, Radio-Tel received a letter from Gretsch stating that the well-established Brooklyn company owned the trademark to the model name. Gretsch "Broadkaster" banjos and drums (with a "k" in place of the "c") had been on the market since the 1920s and were still available at the time of the Fender Broadcaster's release. Not eager to go to court with one of the big boys, Don Randall urged Fender to pull the Broadcaster name from the headstock and from all advertising immediately. Leo conceded.

The event marks the end of the short-lived model, in name at least. Accounts differ on how many Broadcasters were produced from around spring of 1950 to February 1951, but *Gruhn's Guide to Vintage Guitars* estimates three hundred to five hundred, although several accounts indicate that the tally could total fewer than two hundred guitars.[20]

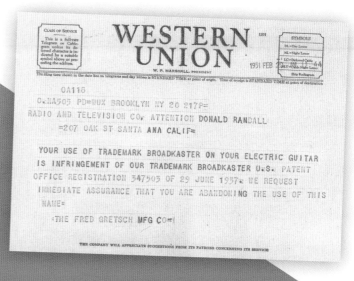

WESTERN UNION
W. P. MARSHALL, PRESIDENT   1951 FEB 21

OA118

O NA505 PD=WUX BROOKLYN NY 20 217P=

RADIO AND TELEVISION CO. ATTENTION DONALD RANDALL
=207 OAK ST SANTA ANA CALIF=

YOUR USE OF TRADEMARK BROADKASTER ON YOUR ELECTRIC GUITAR
IS INFRINGEMENT OF OUR TRADEMARK BROADKASTER U.S. PATENT
OFFICE REGISTRATION 347505 OF 29 JUNE 1937. WE REQUEST
IMMEDIATE ASSURANCE THAT YOU ARE ABANDONING THE USE OF THIS
NAME=

=THE FRED GRETSCH MFG CO=

The change seemed to induce some panic at Fender Sales initially. In a letter to Fender dealers dated February 21, 1951, Don Randall concludes, "It is a shame that our efforts in both selling and advertising are lost . . . . If any of you have a good name in mind I would welcome hearing from you immediately."

To keep production rolling, Fender initially snipped the "Broadcaster" model name from its existing "Fender" head-stock decals, leading to a couple months' worth of guitars that came to be known as the now highly collectible "Nocasters." Precise dates for the Broadcaster-Nocaster-Telecaster transition are difficult to come by, given available early Fender production and shipping records and the dates applied to actual guitars. Most accounts agree that Randall devised the new Telecaster name in April 1951—taking Fender's debut electric Spanish model from the radio age into the television age—and that guitars wearing "Fender Telecaster" decals were hitting the stores by May 1951.

OPPOSITE TOP AND BOTTOM: An early 1951 Nocaster, with Fender logo but no model name. OPPOSITE CENTER: A mid-'50s white-guard Telecaster. RIGHT: Artists test a black two-pickup Esquire at the factory.

Through the early to late 1950s, other changes to the model included:

- Bridge saddles: The three barrel-shaped steel bridge saddles on the earliest guitars were changed to brass saddles around the fall of 1950, then steel saddles of a different diameter in the mid-1950s, then threaded steel saddles toward the late 1950s.

- Bridge pickup: While the Broadcaster's bridge pickup was wound with 43-AWG wire, Fender began winding them with thicker 42-AWG wire around the change to the Nocaster and Telecaster (43-AWG would still be used on the neck pickup).

- Pickguard: This changed from lac-quered black fiberboard to Bakelite to white plastic by late 1954.

- Serial number: A move of the stamped-in serial number from the bridge plate to the neck-mounting plate occurred around late 1954.

- String tree and decal: The reposition-ing (and change of) the string tree on the B and high-E strings to further down on the headstock, and subse-quent move of the decal to fit, happened after 1955.

1951 Telecaster with case, accessories, and bill of sale.

In addition, the guitar's neck profile (the shape of its carve) would evolve throughout the decade and beyond, to the extent that guitars of specific years can sometimes be associated with very particular neck shapes. The hue of the standard blond finish changed through these years, too, evolving from a more butterscotch-tinged blond to a translucent white blond.

One rather odd original feature of the model that wasn't changed until 1967, however, was the wiring of its controls. While the complement of a single Volume control, single Tone control, and a three-way switch wired to access neck pickup, both pickups, or bridge pickup seems the obvious and most practical way to go today, it took Fender seventeen years to arrive at that conclusion.

The Broadcaster's three-way switch was originally wired to an unusual tone circuit, while the so-called "Tone Control" really wasn't a Tone control at all. These switch settings, from forward, to middle, to rear, were (1) "deep rhythm," achieved with the neck pickup wired through a tone capacitor; (2) neck pickup alone (no tone control); (3) both pickups, with the "Tone Control" used as a blender control to add the neck pickup to the bridge pickup as desired.

THE CUSTOM TELECASTER

DUAL EIGHT AND ESQUIRE

ESQUIRE — Single Pickup

Telecaster — Dual Pickup

Sensational modern styling, especially designed neck with built-in adjustable tension rod to correct for warpage due to string tension, cutaway body makes possible full chord combinations up to the end of the fret board, new micro adjustable bridge makes possible string adjustments both for action (or fretting) and length, pickups are fully adjustable for desired balance of bass treble, threeway tone switch for lead or take off tone, full concert tone and short duration rhythm tone, compact size for easy playing and portability, professional players say these guitars have faster, easier action than any other guitar they have ever played.

Radio &
Equipme
207 OAK S
SANTA ANA, C

*1951 Telecaster
headstock, hang tag,
and original accessories.*

Later in 1952 the wiring was changed to offer the same "bassy" sound from the neck pickup in the forward switch setting, neck pickup *with* conventional Tone control in the middle, and bridge with Tone control at the rearward position. There was still no position including both pickups—a setting that arrived, with a conventional use of the Tone control on all positions only in 1967. (The three-position switch on the single-pickup Esquire offered (1) preset bassy sound via tone capacitors; (2) conventional Volume and Tone control; (3) bridge pickup through Volume control only (but not the Tone control) for a brighter sound.)

Meanwhile, before the Broadcaster had even lost its name, Leo and company had expanded the template for the solidbody electric guitar to apply the same thinking to a four-string bass guitar. As we shall see, the Precision Bass would have an enormous and cross-genre impact on the sound of popular music.

A white-guard 1957 Telecaster. The headstock displays the new string tree and repositioned logo. Note also the "hyphen" serial number on the neck plate and the steel-saddle bridge.

THIS SPREAD: *Joe Strummer of the Clash (top), Roy Buchanan (right), and Rolling Stone Keith Richards (opposite top) are just a few players inextricably linked to the Telecaster.* **OPPOSITE BOTTOM:** *Aussie Courtney Barnett rocks her left-hand Telecaster. She and sometimes collaborator Kurt Vile prominently featured their Fenders on the cover of Lotta Sea Lice.*

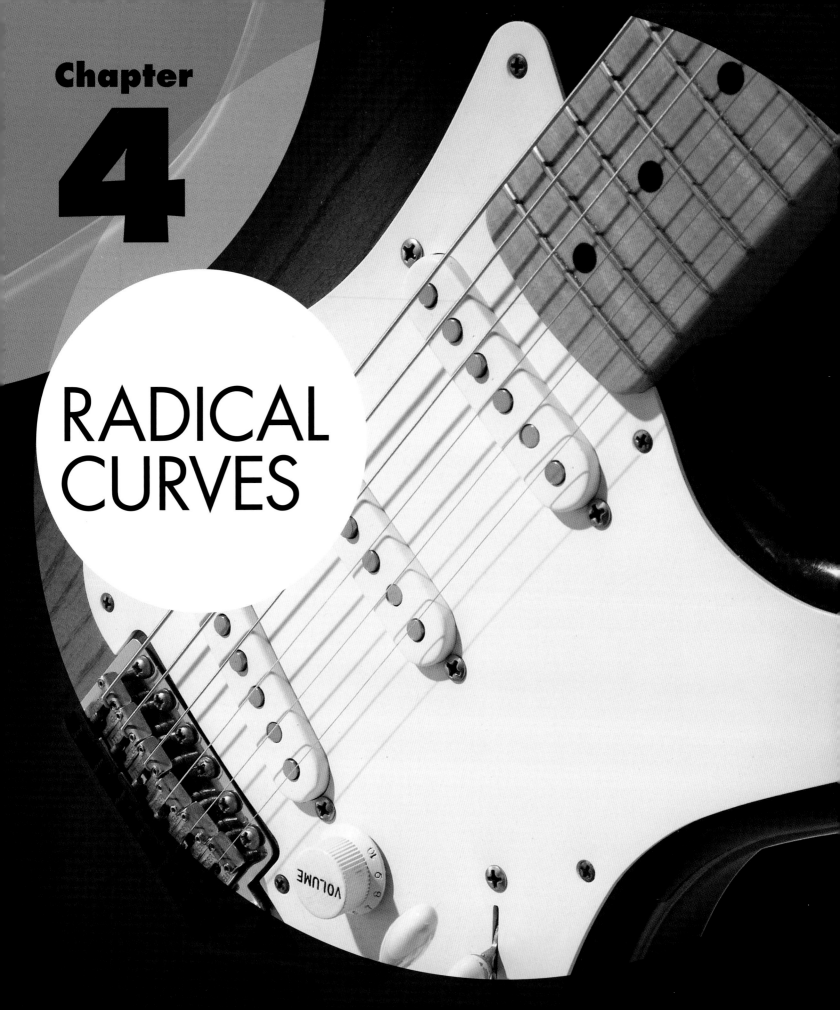

RADICAL CURVES

The Stratocaster and the Precision Bass

Even after seventy-five years of ground-breaking product developments, Fender's back-to-back introduction of the Telecaster and Stratocaster remains perhaps the most significant one-two punch in the history of the electric guitar. Consider that Fender also sandwiched in the design and release of the Precision Bass—an instrument that some believe has had more impact on the sound of popular music than any other—and we have to score a trio of successes in that brief 1950–1954 period that must rival any three consecutive product debuts by any company in any other industry.

Sticking with the six-strings for a moment, it's truly incredible that, in the span of about three and a half years, Fender followed the most influential electric guitar *up to that time* in the Telecaster with a radically new model in 1954 that would become the most influential electric guitar *of all time—period.*

From our vantage in the twenty-first century, where these two formative Fender designs have been an essential part of the landscape for so long, it's easy to underestimate just what an achievement each guitar represented individually.

The Telecaster might not look particularly radical now, but considered alongside the standard fully hollow archtop electric of its day—with its comfortable maple bolt-on neck, stylized body, and integral bridge and pickup unit—it represented a groundbreaking leap in design at the time. With that in mind, consider the exponentially evolutionary leap forward that the Stratocaster would embody less than four years later.

Where one might naturally have expected Fender to simply upgrade the Telecaster design with the extra pickup and spring-loaded vibrato system that would distinguish the Stratocaster's functionality, Leo and the team boldly left behind any stylistic resemblance to the Telecaster and launched the solid-body concept into the stratosphere. Even today, the Stratocaster looks worlds different from the staid Telecaster of just a few years before. At the time of its release, though, it must have looked like an instrument from another planet.

All that *and* they found time to develop, prototype, and unveil yet another instrument that would change the low end for all time (while keeping amplifier and steel-guitar development apace too).

MAIN:
A detail shot accentuates the Space Age lines of a 1954 Stratocaster.

RIGHT:
The 1954 catalog featuring the Stratocaster on the cover.

The Precision Bass

As has often been noted, Leo Fender was astute at discerning the needs of professional musicians and creating practical tools to help them do their work more efficiently and proficiently. As he told authors Tony Bacon and Barry Moorhouse, "About twenty-five percent of every day was spent with visiting musicians, trying to figure out what would suit their needs best."[21] Leo was particularly effective at helping players of fretted stringed instruments make themselves better heard in a performance environment that was rapidly threatening to drown them out in the late 1940s. It is no exaggeration to say that, in delivering salvation from such a threat, Leo Fender also changed the sound and composition of popular music.

And if the humble guitarist was sinking into the background in the onstage volume wars—drowning in a cacophony of horns and drums—consider the plight of the poor upright bassist, thumping away in the lower register with little hope of cutting through. Leo considered it, and he did something about it.

While laboring night and day to make his groundbreaking solidbody electric guitar float in a wary marketplace, Leo was also burning the midnight oil developing what was arguably an even more revolutionary instrument, one that some have said was even closer to his heart. The effort to create a more efficiently amplifiable bass instrument followed the principles that Fender had already applied to lap-steel guitars and early renditions of the Esquire and Broadcaster. It would result in yet another—if lower-registered—rendition of "the Fender sound."

The pickup was a four-pole unit adapted from the template for the Champion lap-steel, one that had also been adapted for the bridge pickup of the electric Spanish guitar. Likewise, the bass's neck and headstock were clearly just enlarged versions of the six-string neck, and the slab ash body was an enlarged rendition of the now-iconic Telecaster shape, evolved into a double-cutaway design with an added and substantially elongated upper horn that both aided balance when hanging from a strap and allowed playing access right up to the top fret.

The resulting punchy, tight, clear sound, combined with the playability of the relatively slim, fretted neck (when compared to the wide fingerboard and poor upper-register access of an upright double bass), added an entirely new tool to the bassist's arsenal, while also appealing to many guitarists who could now easily switch over to the bass clef without having to learn fingering on a fretless instrument.

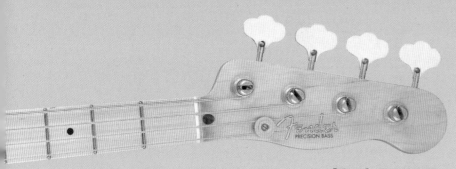

OPPOSITE: *Some argue the Precision Bass has had more impact on popular music than any other instrument.* BELOW: *The Precision Bass patent drawings filed November 21, 1952.*

March 24, 1953

C. L. FENDER

Des. 169,062

GUITAR

Filed Nov. 21, 1952

FIG. 1.

FIG. 2.

FIG. 3.

FIG. 4.

INVENTOR.
CLARENCE L. FENDER
BY
Lyon & Lyon
ATTORNEYS

While Don Randall had named the Esquire and Broadcaster, and would contribute model names to many other significant Fender creations in the future, it was an engineer's love of exact tolerances that led Leo to provide the moniker for this one.

Randall told the story of how the bass got its name:

> Leo and I had a discussion about the new bass, and he's telling me how precise it was, how you could fret it right down to a hundredth of an inch. Now, who puts their finger a hundredth of an inch this way or that on a bass string? But he was so possessed with the fact that this was the first time that the fret layout on a bass was so precise. He said to me, "You know, it's so precise we ought to call it the Precision Bass." Well, why not? So it became the Fender Precision Bass.[22]

SHIFTE HENRI says "MY *Fender* BASS IS THE MOST"

Shaking up the Low End

The Precision Bass was not just a new kind of bass: it was truly a new instrument unto itself, as confirmed by the many session credit notes over the years, with liner notes listing musicians as playing "Fender Bass" rather than merely "Bass." Also noteworthy is how quickly the patent for the Precision Bass came through: while it often took several years to grant patents in the 1940s and 1950s, Fender's patent, filed November 21, 1952, was awarded March 24, 1953. It had taken three and a half years to award Fender and Kauffman their patent for the "strings-through-coil" pickup in the 1940s, and more than four years for Gibson's humbucker (hence its colloquial name, "PAF," for "patent applied for")

to receive its patent at the end of the 1950s. It's impossible to say whether the Precision Bass's status as a new and unique product speeded the process, though that is one possible explanation for the unusually swift action of a normally sluggish federal agency.

Leo's vision of the Precision Bass converting legions of upright jazz bassists to the new fretted, horizontal instrument never fully came to pass, however. It took some time for the Precision Bass to take hold in the western swing and, eventually, rock 'n' roll genres, and it never quite replaced the double bass in jazz outfits—those playing swing and bebop, at least—though it would later proliferate in modern jazz and jazz fusion.

One of the first prominent proponents of the Precision Bass was not a bassist but star vibraphonist and bandleader Lionel Hampton. Hampton insisted his bassist, Roy Johnson, use the Fender not long after it came out, and the instrument

was passed along to a more famous sideman, William "Monk" Montgomery (brother of guitarist Wes Montgomery) when he took over the low end for Hampton later in 1952. Montgomery is also considered the first prominent musician to have recorded with the instrument, using it in sessions with Art Farmer in 1953 before taking it back into the studio with Hampton later that year.

The Precision Bass made a few other inroads into the jazz scene of the 1950s, notably in the hands of John Willie "Shifty" Henry, who, like Montgomery, would appear in Fender ads (as "Shifte Henri") later in the decade. Regardless of the lukewarm uptake in that community, however, the firm, punchy sound of the fretted solidbody bass through an amplifier would dramatically change popular music over the next two decades and become far and away the standard in just about everything other than the more traditional jazz outfits.

OPPOSITE LEFT:
Employees test new 1951 Precision basses.
OPPOSITE RIGHT:
Jazz bassist John Willie "Shifty" Henry appeared in Fender ads (as "Shifte Henri").
RIGHT: *"Monk" Montgomery (brother of guitarist Wes Montgomery) was one of the first prominent musician to record with the Precision Bass. He's seen here in a period ad and as bassist with Lionel Hampton.*

Space Cowboys

The Esquire and Broadcaster, soon dubbed Telecaster, weren't long out of the gate, with the Precision Bass hot on their heels, when Leo started R&D on a new six-string model intended to push the envelope even further. Bountiful artist input and his awareness of other instruments on the market spurred the need for something a little more dramatically styled and more fully featured. When the idea first began percolating, however, it was still difficult to say exactly what that might be.

Leo Fender said in later interviews that he had the basic concept for the new model in place in 1951, and that he had already hammered out the basic format and features without any input from others who have often been credited with contributing. But a tendency to misremember some dates, and a propensity to withhold credit where credit was due, might have played a part in that claim. George Fullerton later said that Leo "never gave credit to anybody. There were very few things in my entire life that Leo gave me credit for personally or ever said, 'Hey, you're doing a good job.'"[23]

Several other parties on the scene concur regarding somewhat later starting and prototyping dates for what would become the Stratocaster. They give credible accounts of their own roles, so we might need to be cautious about some of Leo's claims.

Guitarist Bill Carson, who played with Spade Cooley, Hank Thompson, Wade Ray, and others, was an early proponent of the Telecaster. But his acquisition of the instrument also led him to play a significant role in the development of Fender's next revolutionary six-string design. Unable to purchase a guitar and amp from Leo outright, the pair agreed to a deal in which Carson would pay Fender $18 a month for a Telecaster and a Pro amp while acting as a test pilot for the new product in development. At first, it seemed the arrangement might be more of a nuisance than a benefit to the hard-working musician, but he would eventually find a way to inject several of his ideas into the Fender R&D engine.

"Later meetings turned into months of several hours daily at the shop, plus taking prototype amps to the club where I was working with a band about five hours every night," Carson told Tony Bacon in a 1992 interview.

> The prototypes were crude and rarely had numbers to reference on the faceplate for tone, volume, mid-range, and any other kinds of control they had on them. So it was trial and error for the most part to get the thing set right . . . it took some time, usually about the first set. And it seemed to never fail that as soon as that happened, and I'd got it to what I thought was a pretty good sound, Leo would come in the club. He'd come on up on the bandstand and reset my amp to make it sound "better," or so he thought. And he was just oblivious of other musicians, club management, and disruption generally when he wanted his amplifier to sound better.[24]

As for his take on the Fender six-string, Carson has indicated on several occasions that he urged Leo to make changes to the Telecaster almost from the first time he picked it up. He said in several interviews that he often suggested Fender build a guitar with a built-in vibrato and is also frequently credited with the idea of contouring the new guitar's body.

As Carson told A. R. Duchossoir in 1988 in interviews for his book *The Fender Stratocaster*, "The thing I didn't like about the Telecaster was the discomfort of it, because I was doing a lot of studio work at the time on the West Coast and sitting down its square edges really dug into my rib."[25]

In one of his own interviews with Carson, gleaned from his years as a writer and editor of *Guitar Player* and reprinted in his excellent tome, *The Stratocaster Chronicles: Celebrating 50 Years of the Fender Strat*, Tom Wheeler quoted Carson as saying, "Leo was receptive to a musician just walking in off the street to talk to him. He seemed to want to pick the head of every player who came around. He'd ask all kinds of questions and be very friendly and make you feel comfortable right away."[26]

That said, Leo himself has also been quoted as saying in interviews with Wheeler, Duchossoir, and elsewhere that the contouring notion came from local guitarist Rex Galleon before it was suggested by Carson. Either way it's likely that multiple recommendations from respected performers helped the idea achieve critical mass with Leo, resulting in the two bandsaw swipes for the tummy and forearm contours that produce the extremely comfortable feel of the Stratocaster body as we know it today.

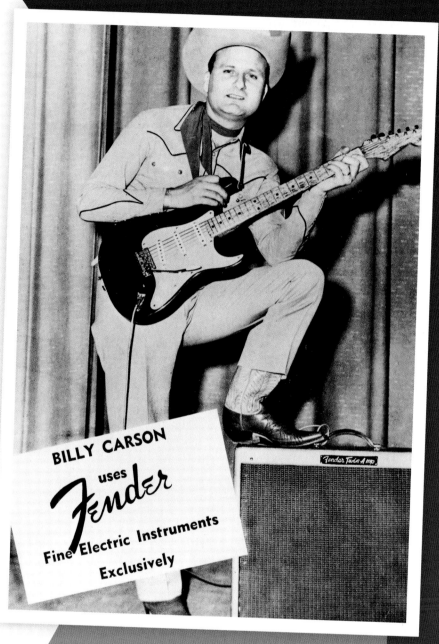

Guitarist Bill Carson played a significant role in the development of the Stratocaster. His 1959 Stratocaster is shown alongside a period ad.

Looney Tunes

Another new member of the Fender design team who purportedly played a role in shoring up the final shape and format of the Stratocaster was Freddie Tavares, a busy Hawaiian-steel player who had come to Los Angeles from his birthplace in Maui several years before. He was the slide player responsible for the iconic *zzzziiing!* opening glissando to the theme tune for the vintage *Looney Tunes* cartoons and had performed on recordings by the Andrews Sisters, Deanna Durbin, Dean Martin, Bing Crosby, the Sons of the Pioneers, and Spike Jones and His City Slickers, and would later even record with Elvis Presley. As if these credits weren't enough, Tavares had taught himself electronics and other mechanical crafts, *and* built his own steel guitars and amplifiers.

While playing at L.A.'s Cowtown Club with the Ozark Mountain Boys in 1953, Tavares was introduced to Leo Fender by fellow steel guitarist Noel Boggs. According to legend, he immediately pointed out several faults in Fender's amps—in answer to which Leo Fender pulled out a screwdriver, removed the back panel from Tavares's own home-made amp, checked the work inside the chassis . . . and offered him a job in the Fender development lab on the spot.[27]

Several accounts from those on the scene during of the development of the Stratocaster indicate that Tavares's job, from day one at Fender, was to concoct the body shape and general design of the new guitar, which was but a basic concept in Leo's mind at the time of Freddie's arrival at the factory in spring 1953. Fender had just moved to a new, larger factory on Pomona Street in Fullerton, and it's clear Leo had much

of the electronics and some rough ideas for the vibrato bridge in place. But other than following the basic double-cutaway lines of the much bigger Precision Bass, the new model had yet to take its final form.

"The first real project that I had was to put the Stratocaster on [the] drawing board," Tavares told Duchossoir. "It was about April or May 1953 and Leo said, 'We need a new guitar,' and I said, 'How far apart are the strings at the nut, how far [at] the bridge?' I got those parameters and I said, 'What's the scale?' Then I knew where the strings are and we started from there."[28]

Carson's memory of developments of 1953 seems to concur. He recalled Leo having roughed-out the desired ribcage and forearm contours on a handful of prototype bodies by early 1953, but these didn't balance properly or hang well on the strap, something he believed Tavares took care of with his final design for the body itself.

Fender Takes Over Sales

The driving force behind sales at Fender, Don Randall had a vested interest in bringing a hot new model to the market and had urged Leo to move forward with the guitar that would become the Stratocaster. Around this time, however, Leo and Radio-Tel owner Francis Hall had a falling-out, and new plans were drawn up for Fender to take sales and distribution in-house. In June 1953 Fender terminated the deal for Radio-Tel to exclusively represent its products, and Randall left his position as Radio-Tel's general manager. Leo Fender and Don Randall formed Fender Sales Inc., of which Randall was made president while also becoming a partner in Fender Electronic Instruments.

Amid all the talk of who-designed-this and who-requested-that in the Stratocaster's development, it's worth remembering that the man responsible for selling Fender instruments, and the team working under him, played an enormous part in the feedback network comprising players, dealers, and maker. Randall was a major font of ideas and an important voice in the design process, ever eager to inspire Leo and the development lab to add original features and those vaunted unique selling propositions (USPs) that could help a guitar salesman get his foot in the door.

It was Randall who had urged Leo to include a truss rod in the Esquire/ Broadcaster neck, an essential ingredient carried over to the Stratocaster and all subsequent Fender guitars, without which Fender's electric Spanish effort would likely have flamed out on the launch pad. Additionally, adjustable bridge saddles, adjustable pickups, multiple pickups with switching, and stylistic elements involving body and headstock shapes might all seem the purview of designers, but as often as not these were concocted at the urging of Randall and his sales team.

For all his undoubted contributions to the effort, though, perhaps the biggest element of the new model for which Randall is widely credited is its name. If the Telecaster model name, also widely attributed to Randall, took the company's debut solidbody from the radio age into the television age, the sales manager—a licensed pilot and avid flyer—would take the new model into the space age by naming it the Stratocaster, thus launching it beyond the present day and into a bold future filled with adventurous music.

FAR LEFT: *The expanded Fender factory in the early 1950s.* LEFT: *At the Fender factory (from left): Don Randall, Leon McAuliffe, unknown, Noel Boggs, and Freddie Tavares.*

Ready to Launch

1954 Stratocaster.

By mid-1953 Fender had Stratocaster prototypes in the field for testing with Bill Carson and others, but little is known of those early efforts. In his book, *Fender: The Sound Heard 'Round The World*, Richard Smith published photos of a supposed Stratocaster prototype from 1953 that were taken by Leo Fender showing a "breadboard" guitar of sorts, with a black fiber pickguard, knurled silver Telecaster-style knobs, and a back rout wide enough to take only three springs rather than the standard five.[29]

Otherwise George Fullerton offered some clue as to why Stratocaster prototypes are so thin on the ground: "Leo Fender was the type of person, soon as a prototype was proven, you'd cut it up and get rid of it, you won't keep it around any longer. So most of the prototypes got cut up and thrown away."[30]

Carson offers yet another explanation for the scarcity of prototypes today:

The original prototype of the Strat was stolen from Fender along with several other early models that were being stored with the expectation of someday having a Fender museum. We always suspected employee theft, but only one of the items has surfaced in the collection that was stolen that I know of. And I get calls from people now and then who think they have discovered my old prototype, but so far nothing. There are certain characteristics and marks on the guitar, some of them inside, some of them stamped in the metal, that only I know about, so it would make it easy to identify if it ever does surface.[31]

Fullerton later recalled that the vibrato bridge was the last part of the design to come into place on the new model, with everything else ready to go and the intention of launching the Stratocaster at the summer NAMM show in 1953. Fender had already started putting one hundred Stratocasters through the line—and had completed one guitar—when Fullerton headed over to production to check them out.

"I grabbed that one and tested it out," said Fullerton, "and it was terribly bad sounding. . . . I rushed to the lab, Leo and I looked at it, and we called Freddie over to look at it. That vibrato sounded like a tin can. We all agreed it wasn't going to work, so we shut down the line. It was a sad day. It was then that Leo went back to the drawing board."[32]

The problem with the vibrato unit, which was in fact an early design of the component that would later find its way to the Jazzmaster, was a lack of mass at the strings' body-end termination points. To compensate, Leo devised a steel inertia block that he mounted below the vibrato's baseplate. The strings were loaded through holes drilled through the block and, as a result, were anchored with the mass needed for satisfactory tone and sustain.

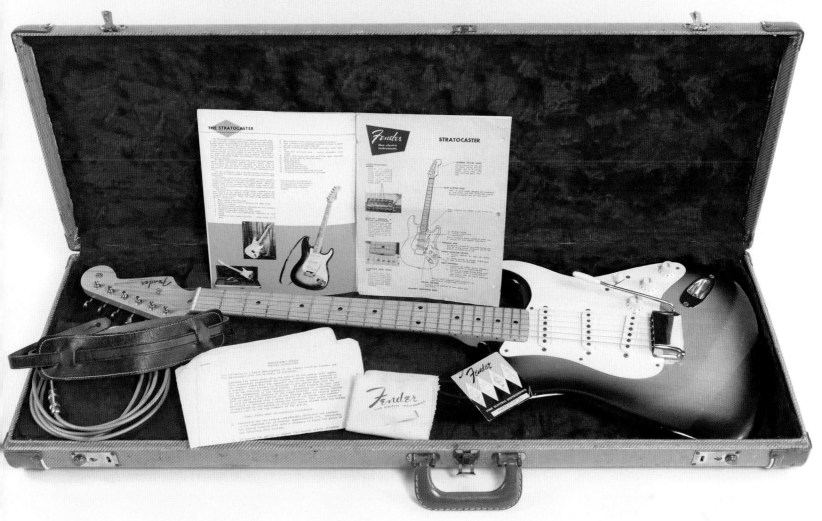

A 1957 Stratocaster with original literature, hang tag, spare strings, and case.

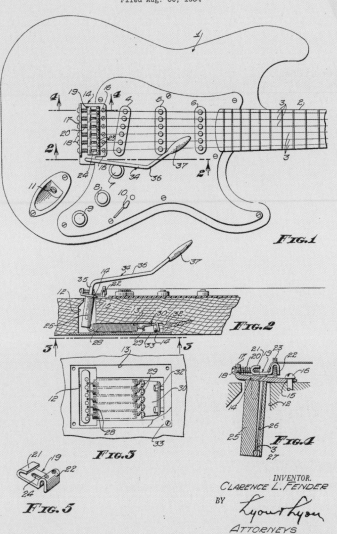

April 10, 1956   C. L. FENDER   2,741,146

TREMOLO DEVICE FOR STRINGED INSTRUMENTS

Filed Aug. 30, 1954

FIG.1

FIG.2

FIG.3

FIG.4

FIG.5

INVENTOR.
CLARENCE L. FENDER

BY *Lyon+Lyon*
ATTORNEYS

ABOVE: *A patent application for the "tremolo" bridge was filed August 30, 1954.* **ABOVE RIGHT:** *A Fender employee puts the finishing touches on a 1950s Stratocaster.* **RIGHT:** *The first Stratocaster ad.* **FAR RIGHT:** *Hank Marvin of the Shadows was the first English guitarist to own a Stratocaster.* **OPPOSITE:** *Employees put new Stratocasters through their paces in 1955.*

Although it put the new model's development back as much as six months, the Stratocaster vibrato bridge was a wonder of engineering, combining adequate mass, an absence of dead string space (and the tuning and inadequate tension issues that can result), and individual saddles adjustable for both height and length into one elegant, compact unit. The original production version of this vibrato bridge—erroneously called a tremolo by Fender at the time—has remained a major selling point of the Stratocaster throughout the seven decades of its existence and has become the most copied vibrato unit of all time. (A patent application for the design was filed August 30, 1954, with the patent granted fewer than two years later.)

Early production Stratocasters began coming off the line in spring 1954, and Fender sales literature announced that "shipments are expected to begin May 15." Given that the new model's specifications settled into place in September or October of that year, when production numbers ramped up even more, Stratocasters manufactured in the late spring and summer of 1954 are sometimes referred to as preproduction models, yet the guitar was already featured in the Fender catalog and advertisements by this time, so "early production models" is probably more accurate.

At the time of its launch, the Stratocaster's retail price was set at $249.50 with Synchronized Tremolo, or $229.50 in the "hardtail" version without the vibrato, plus $39.95 for the case, with the Telecaster at $189.50. Notable features of the new model included the following:

- A larger headstock, purportedly requested by Don Randall to better display the Fender logo

- A more comfortable body shape, with contours where it met the player's ribcage and right forearm

- A broader sonic range, courtesy of three individual pickups, two Tone controls, and a master Volume control

- A more ergonomic control layout, along with a recessed jack for accidental pullout safety

- A built-in vibrato bridge with six bridge saddles individually adjustable for both height and length (a first among large-scale production guitars)

- Stylish, ultramodern looks with two-tone Sunburst finish as standard

While some early models would occasionally be finished in blond or black, custom colors were not yet available (officially at least), although Fender was known to apply them for occasional noteworthy artists.

THE MARY KAYE TRIO uses *Fender* fine electric instruments exclusively

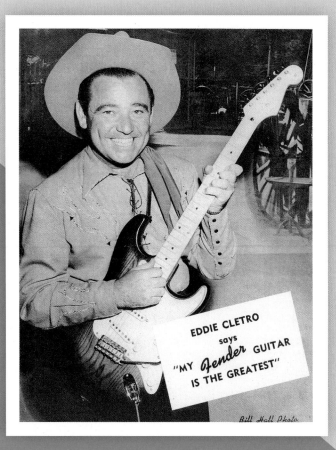

EDDIE CLETRO says "MY *Fender* GUITAR IS THE GREATEST"

Bill Hall Photo

CHARLEY RAYE uses only *Fender* fine electric instruments

BUDDY MERRILL featured guitarist with the Lawrence Welk Orchestra uses only *Fender* Fine Electric Instruments

Star Reception

Somewhat like the Broadcaster and Telecaster before it, the new Stratocaster did not immediately set the guitar world on fire, though it was also less derided than Fender's debut, plank-bodied electric. It was clearly a work of considerable engineering and design prowess, and with rock 'n' roll about to hit the ground running as the hot new musical genre of teens and young adults, the guitar's lithe, sultry lines virtually screamed "Rock me!"

THIS SPREAD: *Early Stratocaster endorsers appear pleased with their instruments.* RIGHT: *Texas Playboys guitarist Eldon Shamblin (far right, with Forrest White, second from right) had scoffed at the Telecaster but eagerly took up a custom-finished gold Stratocaster.*

STASH CLEMENTS
PREFERS
Fender
FINE ELECTRIC INSTRUMENTS

ALVINO REY
prefers
Fender
Fine Electric Instruments

Clearly proud of his role in helping shape the instrument, Bill Carson became one of the first prominent artists to endorse the Stratocaster, in an era when true national guitar heroes were still few and far between (Chet Atkins and Les Paul aside). Carson was seen in ads cradling his early, custom-finished "Cimarron Red" Strat, which often looked black in the monochrome photos of the day. Texas Playboys guitarist Eldon Shamblin, who had scoffed at the Telecaster just a couple years before, eagerly took up another custom-finished gold Stratocaster, while the first real pop idol to take the sultry new Fender model to the nation, Buddy Holly, went through four Stratocasters in his short career between 1955 and his untimely death in 1959.

Buddy Holly was an early adopter of the Stratocaster.

Arguably, though, the full potential of Fender's Stratocaster design wouldn't be revealed until a decade later, when an adventurous, boundary-defying breed of new guitarists used the instrument to produce genre-melding music, creating soundscapes virtually unimaginable at the time of the model's introduction. Most notably Jimi Hendrix probed every nuance of the Strat's tonal capabilities to set new horizons for what the electric guitar could do. In his wake, Ritchie Blackmore applied a Stratocaster to Deep Purple's thundering heavy rock, while Eric Clapton furthered the instrument's approval in the blues camp in the wake of Hendrix, Buddy Guy, and others.

1959 (top) and 1955 (right) Stratocasters. One major feature was its six individually adjustable bridge saddles, a first for a large-scale production guitar.

Throughout the seven decades during which it has reigned, the Fender Stratocaster has continued as the instrument of choice for many of the most groundbreaking musicians ever to play the electric guitar. From Jeff Beck to Yngwie Malmsteen, Ike Turner to Rory Gallagher, Mark Knopfler to David Gilmour, Eddie Hazel to Eric Johnson, Adrien Belew to Richard Thompson, and on and on through more virtuosic performers than we'd have room to recount, the Stratocaster has been proven over and over again the most versatile instrument ever conceived.

TOP: *Deep Purple's Ritchie Blackmore brought the Stratocaster to heavy rock.* **BOTTOM:** *Bonnie Raitt and her road-worn 1965 Stratocaster.*

TOP: *Jimi Hendrix probed every nuance of the Strat's tonal capabilities.*
BOTTOM: *Bluesmen extraordinaire Buddy Guy and Eric Clapton put their Stratocasters through the paces.*

"This guitar is rock 'n' roll. It's sexy. It has that whole thing—it's lustful."

ERIC CLAPTON (re the Stratocaster)
Curves, Contours and Body Horns, ITV
December 1994

THE NEED
FOR TWEED

Fender Amps of the Fifties

Considering the groundbreaking triple threat that Fender landed with the Telecaster, Precision Bass, and Stratocaster before the 1950s had even hit their halfway point, it's all too easy to lose track of the advances that Leo and the team were making in amplifier development. While most companies manufacturing both guitars and amps in that era tried to sell them as sets, the reputation of Fender amplifiers was outpacing that of its electric Spanish guitars in the mid-1950s, and they were becoming regarded as the most robust and best-sounding available.

"The amplifiers were the biggest volume item," Don Randall recalled several years later, "then the standard [Spanish] guitars, and then the steel guitars—this was after the big steel guitars school thing began to decline."[33]

Fender had already established a major presence in the guitar amp world by the end of the 1940s, when players were plugging their Gibson, Epiphone, Gretsch, and other big-bodied archtop electric guitars into amplifiers manufactured by Fender to pair with lap-steels before the company even had an electric Spanish guitar of its own. Leo and the team had already displayed their pro-grade chops with the release of the groundbreaking Dual Professional combo in 1946 (see Chapter Two), soon known as the Super. As the company came roaring into the 1950s, it would position itself as a leading innovator in the amplifier market, even though it was still a relatively small company in the industry.

Looking back in 1978, Leo said, "One successful amplifier was the first Super. You know, Fender's had the Super amplifier in one form or another for, what—thirty years now? More than that, I guess. The first one was unique. It had twin speakers—pretty unusual in those days, although you might not think so now. And we had them arranged so that if you looked at the amplifier from the top, the front of it had a V shape; the speakers were angled to give you wide dispersion."[34]

MAIN:
A tweed Champ in an ideal role as dressing-room practice amp.

RIGHT:
Fender X-rayed a high-powered Twin amplifier to show how well the amp was constructed.

THE INSIDE STORY

Why X-Ray an amplifier? True, an X-Ray doesn't show you what Fender Amps can really do, but we wanted the opportunity of showing you why Fender Amps are the best choice for musicians everywhere. First, they are constructed of only the finest components, sturdily enclosed in a rugged, heavy-duty cabinet built for hard professional use. The components of a Fender Amp, such as the heavy-duty power and output transformers and distortion-free Jensen speakers provide longer Amp life. In addition, the distinctive abrasion-resistant luggage linen covering and convenient top-mounted controls give these amps a beautifully finished appearance.

To find out how Fender Amps can really perform, visit your Fender Dealer today . . . try them . . . listen and compare. You'll prove to yourself that Fender Amps have the finest overall tone quality and will give you trouble-free top performance.

WHEN YOU BUY FENDER, YOU BUY QUALITY FROM THE INSIDE OUT!

Fender
SANTA ANA, CALIF.

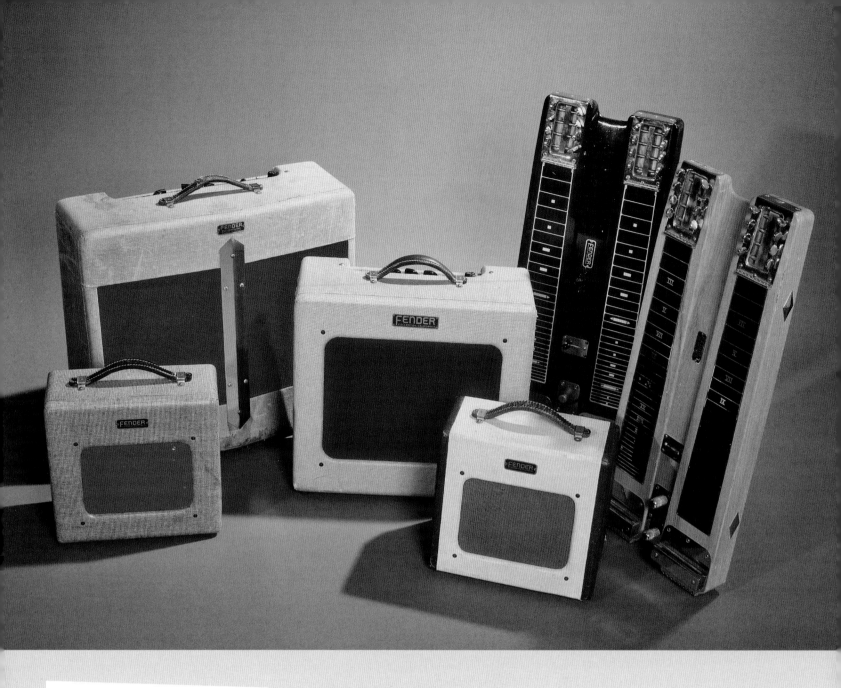

From TV-Front to Bassman

When the 1940s rolled into the 1950s, the full Fender amplifier lineup included the Champion, Princeton, Deluxe, Super, and Pro. All amps other than the V-front Super were housed in the so-called "TV-front" cabinets that Fender had moved to after the demise of the early woodie cabs. So called for their resemblance to early television sets, TV-fronts had a screen-shaped window of brown-linen grille cloth showing front and center between wide cabinet panels on all four sides. All but the entry-level Champ were covered in aircraft-grade linen, a.k.a. tweed, the name that has

come to define Fender amps of this era. (The little Champ had its own two-tone, cream-and-brown leatherette covering.)

Despite the late-1940s cosmetic holdovers, the entire Fender amp range displayed some of the most advanced design considerations in the business. The folded-steel chassis, top-of-cab control panel positioning (again, in all but the Champ), the use of circuit boards throughout the range, and finger-jointed pine cabinets were all state of the art and bolstered Fender's reputation.

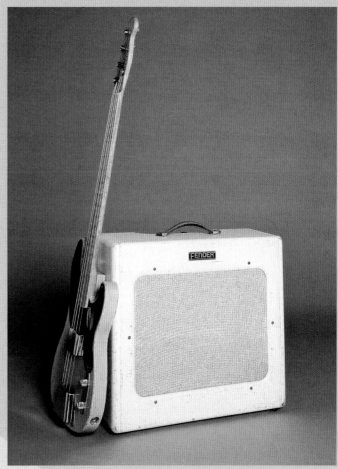

The first notable new introduction to the amp lineup of the early 1950s was arguably a new combo intended to partner with Fender's revolutionary new bass. When the Precision Bass came out in 1951, Fender had yet to offer a proper bass amplifier; in the early months of its existence, the bass most often was paired with the 1x15-inch Pro.

A Fender sales flier printed in 1952 to promote the Precision Bass, however, shows the instrument leaning against a new combo amp listed only as "Amplifier." The unnamed amp has a 1x15-inch TV-front cabinet; a smaller inset photo shows that the amp's rear is mostly enclosed by a solid panel with two circular ports to enhance the bass response. The amp was also unusual in the Fender lineup in that it had a main chassis mounted at the bottom of the cabinet, with an umbilical cord of wires connecting it to a control panel at the top of the cab. Once again, the product name would come courtesy of Don Randall: "I tried to get names that I felt were indicative of what the instrument did or performed . . . so, the Bassman."[35]

One of the more short-lived configurations, the Bassman soon migrated into Fender's elegant new "wide-panel" tweed cabinet in late 1952 or early 1953. It would change more dramatically later in the decade (as we shall see), with another enduring and legendary Fender amplifier leading the way.

OPPOSITE: *A Princeton, Super, Pro, and Champ from the 1950 TV-front amp lineup alongside two double-neck steel guitars.*
ABOVE LEFT: *A cased-up Broadcaster leans on an early TV-front Bassman and two-tone Champ.* ABOVE RIGHT: *Fender Precision Bass and 1952 Bassman combo.*

A Twin Is Born and
Bring on the Bandmaster

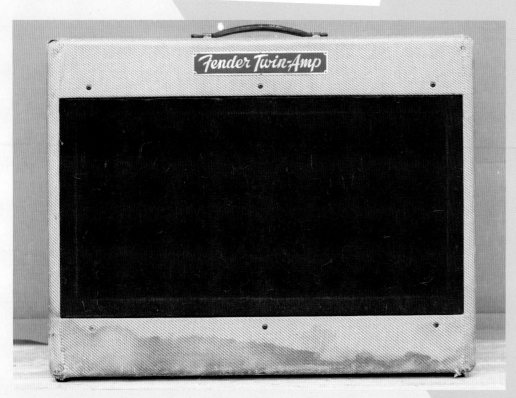

As amplified popular music grew ever louder on stage, guitarists were in need of even more firepower—and greater fidelity to go with it. The goal of Leo Fender and other amp designers in the industry was clear, *undistorted* music power. That many blues and rock 'n' roll players would soon discover the glories of a cranked-up tweed Fender amp singing and wailing well into the overdrive zone was a different matter, but for Fender in the 1950s, maximum headroom was the name of the game.

Fender made major strides in this direction at the summer 1952 NAMM show with the introduction of what would become the Twin combo, one of the most iconic guitar amps of all time. Initially displayed enigmatically as a new "hi-fidelity" amplifier, then dubbed the "Twin 12 Amplifier" by the time new fliers and catalogs were printed, this big combo carried two 12-inch Jensen speakers along with an impressive new EQ stage that offered both Bass and Treble controls. For a few years, the Twin retained dual output tubes rather than the powerful quartet of 6L6s that would later double its output capabilities in the form of the 80-watt "high-powered" Twin of 1958. At the time of its introduction, the Twin likely put out 25 to 35 watts at most, but that was a lot of oomph in its day.

In the cosmetics department, the Twin was the first Fender amp produced in the new "wide-panel" cabinet, which dispensed with the full-front fascia around the speaker grille, replacing it with upper and lower panels to which the baffle was affixed. In 1953 the entire amplifier line moved to the new cabinet style, although the Champ remained a little different, with an upper rear-mounted control panel. Meanwhile all models continued to evolve fairly rapidly as Fender introduced circuit changes throughout the range to improve power, fidelity, and tone-shaping options.

OPPOSITE: *A 1954 Twin Amp, Fender's first with independent Bass and Treble controls.* ABOVE: *Al Myers promotes the Stratocaster and Twin Amp in an ad circa 1954.* RIGHT: *Fender's most deluxe gear circa 1953: the Bandmaster and Twin amps and four-neck console steel.*

LISTEN!

"Sure sounds better than a Gibson!"

Fender Twin-Amp

THE FINEST musical instrument amplification

Your choice of
eleven models:

Twin Amp
Bassman Amp
Bandmaster Amp
Pro Amp
Super Amp
Tremolux Amp
Vibrolux Amp
Deluxe Amp
Harvard Amp
Princeton Amp
Champ Amp

COMPARISON WILL PROVE FENDER'S SUPERIORITY!

Fender
SALES, INC.

SOLD BY LEADING MUSIC DEALERS EVERYWHERE!   Santa Ana, California

Hot on the heels of unveiling the full wide-panel line, Fender released another new amp that was a mainstay for years, albeit one that would change shape and format perhaps more than any other enduring model. Ahead of the 1953 NAMM show at the Palmer House hotel in Chicago, Fender posted a full-page ad in *The Music Trades* publicizing the Twin amp, a new console steel guitar (a lap-steel on legs) with four eight-string necks, and the new Bandmaster amp. Although the Bandmaster was a dual-6L6 1x15-inch combo just like the Pro (and the Bassman, for that matter), it boasted the new independent Bass and Treble controls that had been introduced on the Twin the year before, further paving the way for more powerful tone stages on the larger amps in the Fender lineup.

The fact that specifications for the same model changed, in some cases, over a period of several months is a testament to just how rapidly Fender was innovating

ABOVE: *Don't try this at home: a young music fan soaks up the high-powered Twin's 85-plus watts in this 1959 ad.* RIGHT: *Fender workers often signed their completed work on masking tape inside the amplifier's chassis. Here Lupe Lopez left her mark inside a Twin.* OPPOSITE TOP: *A factory worker wires up the chassis of a wide-panel Deluxe.* OPPOSITE BOTTOM: *A 1953 Pro in new wide-panel tweed cabinet.*

in the amp department throughout the 1950s. With no new professional-grade electric Spanish guitars released between 1954 and 1958 (the new student models of the mid 1950s notwithstanding; see Chapter Six), this really was a period of intensive R&D from the electronics team, building toward significant advances that would deliver some of the most respected and desirable amps of all time in the late 1950s. Before the end of the wide-panel era, Fender amps would lose their octal (eight-pin) preamp tubes in favor of new nine-pin 12AY7, 7025, and 12AX7 tubes that produced less heat while also being less microphonic.

Even the wide-panel cabinets were short-lived, lasting only about two years, but the new styling that replaced them would accompany a line of amps that have become synonymous with tweed for players who have coveted their sound for more than six decades.

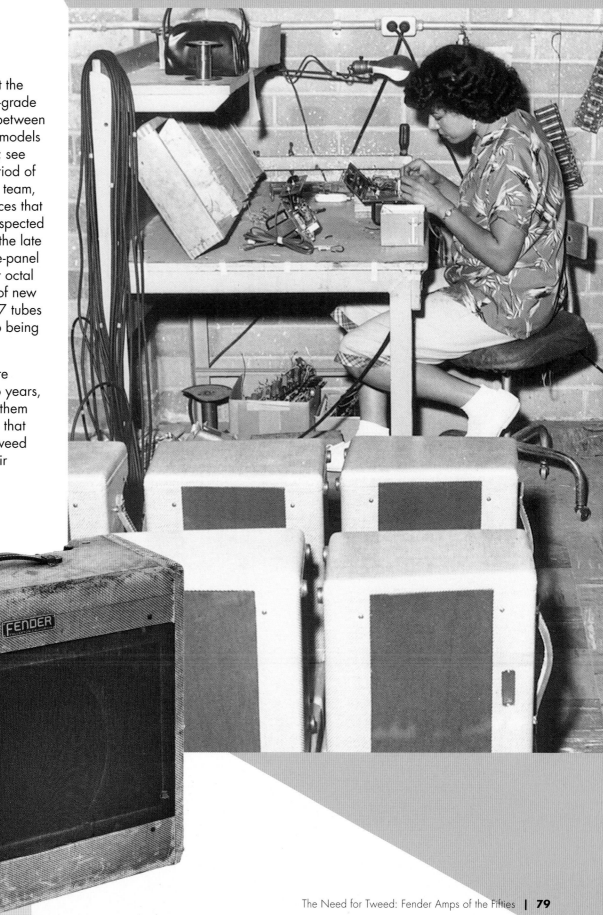

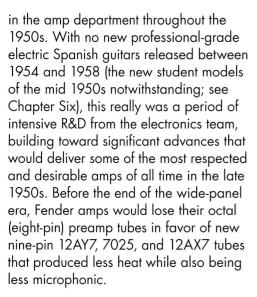

Narrow Panel Cabs and Classic Combos

In 1955 Fender gave its entire amplifier lineup a svelte and stylish new cabinet design. Forever after known as the "narrow-panel" cabs, these finger-jointed, solid-pine cabinets had considerably narrower mounting panels at the top and bottom of the box's front, to which the speaker baffle was affixed. The baffles were now covered in the first real speaker-grille cloth that Fender ever used—a woven plastic fabric that wouldn't impede soundwaves—and had a new script logo plate affixed at the center of the upper panel, replacing the archaic block Fender logo of the wide-panel amps.

While remaining much the same on the outside, models kept evolving internally at a rapid pace over the next few years, gradually taking on significant upgrades that would come to define what many players feel constituted the best specs of the company's 1950s tweed amps.

As the narrow-panel lineup settled into itself, all the larger amps in the range acquired independent Bass and Treble controls. They also gained a more efficient and powerful output-stage configuration, with the Super, Pro, Bandmaster, Twin, and Bassman losing their cathode-biasing in favor of a fixed-bias setup for their 6L6s or 5881s. The change also meant that Fender could add Presence controls to each of these amps, allowing for fine tuning of the high frequencies at the output stage.

"That was a real popular thing," Leo recalled many years later. "Really, what it did was, it took the place of the Bright switch that we used later. You know, most amplifiers don't have such a good response in the higher frequency ranges, and we felt the guitar player should have the option of giving that treble a little extra boost."[36]

BELOW LEFT: *A 1956 narrow-panel Pro.*
BELOW RIGHT: *A 1956 narrow-panel Deluxe.*
OPPOSITE TOP: *A brochure details Fender's new narrow-panel lineup.* OPPOSITE BOTTOM: *The back of a 1959 Tremolux. Housed in a Pro-sized cabinet, this 18-watter emulated Fender's designs for larger amps.*

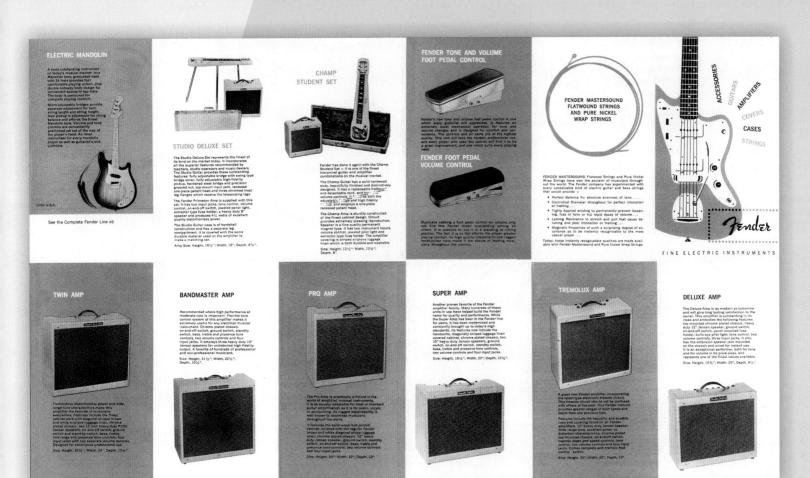

ELECTRIC MANDOLIN

CHAMP STUDENT SET

STUDIO DELUXE SET

FENDER TONE AND VOLUME FOOT PEDAL CONTROL

FENDER FOOT PEDAL VOLUME CONTROL

FENDER MASTERSOUND FLATWOUND STRINGS AND PURE NICKEL WRAP STRINGS

ACCESSORIES GUITARS AMPLIFIERS COVERS CASES STRINGS

Fender

FINE ELECTRIC INSTRUMENTS

See the Complete Fender Line at:

TWIN AMP

BANDMASTER AMP

PRO AMP

SUPER AMP

TREMOLUX AMP

DELUXE AMP

Entirely new to the mid-sized lineup of 1955 was the Tremolux, an 18-watt, dual-6V6, 1x12 combo with built-in bias-modulated tremolo, a first for Fender. Although it debuted in the same smaller cabinet that housed the Deluxe, a couple years later the Tremolux moved up into the larger cabinet that housed the Pro (though it retained its 12-inch speaker), while gaining other circuit refinements. A change to a long-tailed-pair phase inverter and fixed-bias output stage—a combination elsewhere found only in Fender's two largest amps of 1958–1960—would make the 5G9 Tremolux the "biggest-sounding smaller Fender tweed amp" in the eyes and ears of many players.

Roaring Deluxe to 4×10 Bassman

Even though the smaller amps remained less complex, the narrow-panel era of 1955–1960 ushered in one of the all-time classic tone machines of the sub-20-watt range: the 5E3 Deluxe. Able to be driven into juicy, dynamic overdrive at reasonable volume levels, yet still plenty loud for toothsome clean playing in club-sized venues, the archetypal tweed Deluxe is an iconic lower-powered rock 'n' roll and blues amp, and has been a Fender favorite in reissue form decades after its birth.

Meanwhile that odd duck born late in 1952 as a partner to the Precision Bass was rapidly evolving through the narrow-panel years to become arguably the most revered and influential rock 'n' roll, blues, and even rock amp, of all time. In order to halt the service and warranty nightmare of one blown 15-inch speaker after another, Fender figured out in 1955 that four 10-inch speakers could handle the robust thrust of a Precision Bass's low-E much better than a single 15-inch, introducing the narrow-panel 5E6 model in that configuration.

Along with the change in speakers, the Bassman's circuit was substantially upgraded, making it not only a better bass amp, but a killer guitar amp as well. According to Bill Carson, "The 4×10 Bassman was entirely Freddie Tavares's design. Leo was working on something else at the time. Freddie put his thing together. The attempt was to make it kind of a two-edged-sword bass amp that guitar players could use, too, so it could fulfill two roles and make it more acceptable to the buying public. It was also the choice of harmonica players for a long time."[37]

Over the next few years, the Bassman gained a long-tailed-pair phase inverter in place of the cathodyne (a.k.a. split-load) inverter. It was the first Fender amp to attain this more advanced link between preamp and output stages, further increasing its headroom and fidelity. Soon it picked up a Middle control as well.

1958-59 CATALOG

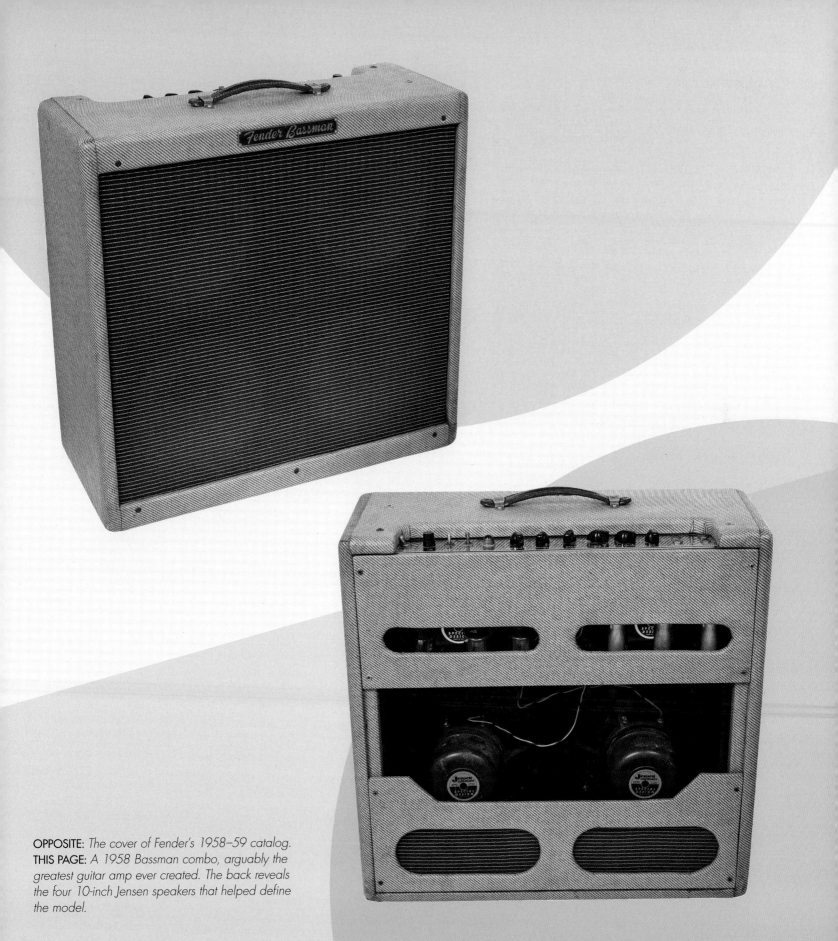

OPPOSITE: The cover of Fender's 1958–59 catalog.
THIS PAGE: A 1958 Bassman combo, arguably the greatest guitar amp ever created. The back reveals the four 10-inch Jensen speakers that helped define the model.

THUMBS CARLLILE
prefers
Fender
Fine Electric Instruments

In 1958 the Bassman hit its final form as the legendary 5F6-A, with all the above features plus a sturdy GZ34 rectifier tube. Six-stringers quickly discovered what the punchy, meaty combo had to offer and it won a following with legions of professional guitarists as well as bassists. Early proponents like Strat-playing country artist Thumbs Carllile and rising rock 'n' roll star Buddy Holly helped take the 4×10-inch Bassman to the masses, while Buddy Guy, Jimmie and Stevie Ray Vaughan, Bruce Springsteen, Mike McCready of Pearl Jam, Joe Bonamassa,

and many others have enshrined its glories through the years. Many players and collectors alike consider it the finest guitar amplifier ever built.

In the early 1960s, again proving that imitation is the sincerest form of flattery, Jim Marshall and his team in London used the 5F6-A circuit as the template for their own British-built rock amp, the JTM45. As a result, a little bit of tweed Bassman DNA lingered through several evolutions of Marshall amps.

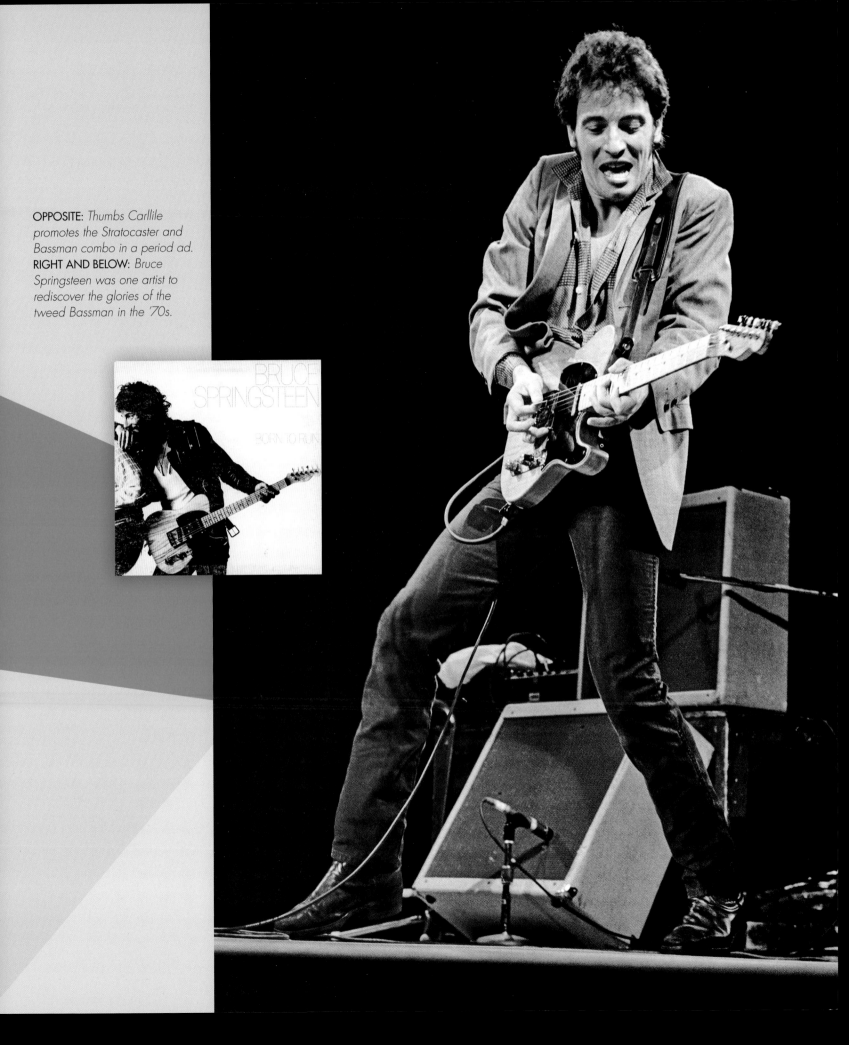

OPPOSITE: *Thumbs Carllile promotes the Stratocaster and Bassman combo in a period ad.*
RIGHT AND BELOW: *Bruce Springsteen was one artist to rediscover the glories of the tweed Bassman in the '70s.*

ALL
THAT
JAZZ

Offset Guitars and Upmarket Advertising

As Fender roared through the mid-1950s, the company made a concerted effort to move its image upmarket while expanding the lineup with new models. The covers of the 1955 and 1956 catalogs were notably more stylish than those of previous years, but the PR endeavors of Don Randall and the team at Fender Sales improved exponentially before the end of the decade with the help of a creative and keen-eyed young advertising agent.

Meanwhile in 1956 Fender saw the benefit in adding two new student models to the electric Spanish guitar lineup to lure entry-level players to the brand, while working toward releasing an entirely new professional-grade model nearer the end of the decade, logging what most would consider the company's third genuine six-string classic.

You Won't Part with Yours Either

You won't part with yours either*

Where musicians go, you'll find Fender!

* For your personal selection see the complete line of Fender fine electric instruments (like the famous "Stratocaster" guitar shown above) on display at leading music dealers throughout the world.

Fender
SALES INC.

308 EAST FIFTH ST. • SANTA ANA. CALIF.

THIS AND NEXT SPREAD:
The Perine/Jacoby "You won't part with yours either" campaign was unfailingly stylish and appealing. The funeral ad (bottom center, page 90) was never released, as sales head Don Randall found it too morbid.

In 1957 Robert Perine and Ned Jacoby had only been operating their small advertising agency for a year when they got a call from Fender Sales and began a promotional campaign that would become the most iconic in the history of musical instrument advertising.

Perine had learned to play the guitar a little while serving in the navy in World War II, and the pair had been hired to do an ad for Rickenbacker for *The Music Trades* shortly after escaping the smog of L.A. and setting up shop in coastal Newport Beach south of the city. When he took the call from Fender sales executive Stan Compton, Perine had never heard of the Fender company, but the idea of logging an account with a guitar company piqued his interest, and the small agency needed the business.

"So, the Fender phone call appeared to be providential," Perine said in 2003, "and I was soon being instructed in the fine points of the solidbody electric by the likes of Compton and Don Randall, chief of Fender Sales. In 1957, my ad designs for Fender began appearing regularly in *Music Trades*, *Downbeat*, and one or two other publications, and by catalog time in 1958 I'd convinced Compton we should at least have a full-color cover on their major sales tool, the yearly product catalog."[38]

The ad campaign launched by Perine/Jacoby featured a series of artfully photographed scenarios in which "guitarists"

took their Fender guitars and amps into unusual situations, headed by a kicker of a strap line: "You won't part with yours either." The results were unfailingly stylish and appealing, and conjured then contemporary vignettes that did wonders to lift Fender's profile and reputation.

Over several years of the relationship between Fender and Perine/Jacoby, the campaign displayed a cowboy carrying a Telecaster and a narrow-panel Twin amp on a busy city sidewalk, a scuba diver carrying his Strat and amp into the sea, a skydiver plummeting—pre-chute opening—with a Jazzmaster around his neck, and several other fanciful scenarios. Just a few years into the campaign, Fender's sales had increased by leaps and bounds.

"During the early 1960s," Perine said, "Fender guitars and amps caught fire, with our ads and collateral materials lending a steady boost to the process. A backlog of orders stacked up. Randall and Compton emphasized the teenage market was of vital importance because kids in every major city were being encouraged by dealers to take guitar lessons, so I slanted many of the ads towards them, going to teenage fairs in southern California, finding teen models, putting them in situations where the guitars looked user-friendly."[39]

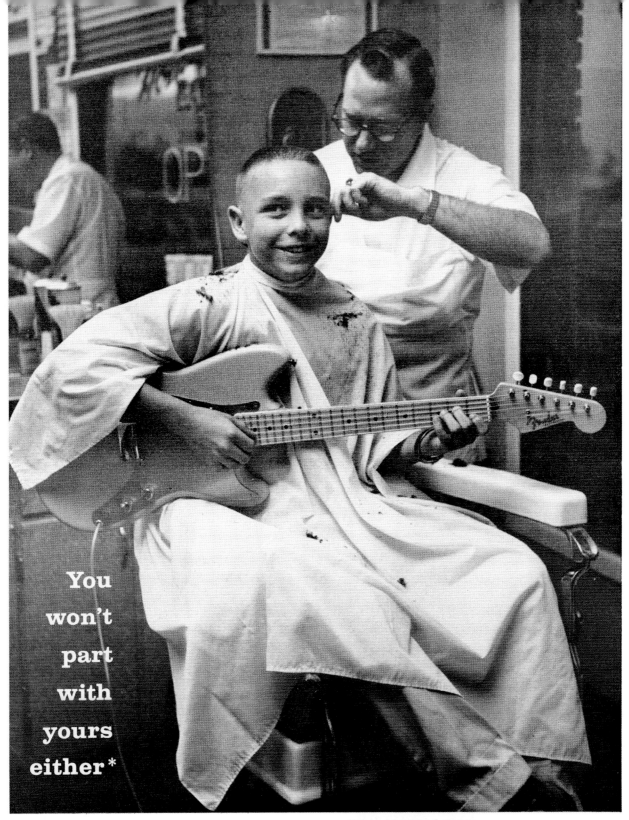

You
won't
part
with
yours
either*

Where musicians go, you'll find Fender!

*To help you select the finest instrument available for the young student your leading music dealer has a complete line of Fender Fine Electric Instruments (like the three-quarter size "Musicmaster" guitar shown above)

SALES INC.

308 EAST FIFTH ST. • SANTA ANA, CALIF.

You won't part with yours either*

You won't part with yours either*

You won't part with yours either*

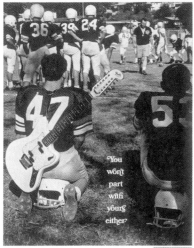

You won't part with yours either

You won't part with yours either*

You won't part with yours either*

You won't part with yours either

You won't part with yours either*

You won't part with yours either*

Student Models and Precision Revisions

The Perine/Jacoby advertising efforts often featured guitar models that Fender had introduced a year or two earlier to reach an entry-level market. First off the bench in 1956, the Musicmaster was a simple guitar with a body that looked like a scaled-down Stratocaster, a single pickup in the neck position, and a shorter 22½-inch scale length. A few months later Fender released the Duo-Sonic, which was entirely the same apart from the inclusion of two pickups and a three-way toggle switch selector.

Often referred to as "three-quarter-sized guitars," you only need to do the math to work out that the 22½-inch scale length is closer to ⅞ the size of Fender's 25½-inch standard. Even so the scale reduction of 3 inches and the downsizing of the rest of the design did indeed help these models appeal to smaller players, while their significantly lower pricing when compared to the Telecaster and Stratocaster made them accessible to grownup players who simply couldn't afford the bigger Fenders.

Just before unveiling the student models, Fender had brought a few changes to the Precision Bass heading into 1955. Following the design success of its contoured body, the Stratocaster returned the favor, transmuting its softened ribcage and forearm curves to the four-string. Fender also changed the early pressed-fiber string saddles to steel saddles and began offering the bass in a two-tone Sunburst similar to the Stratocaster's finish.

In 1957 Leo designed a new pickup for the Precision Bass, for which he would later receive a patent. The split design incorporates two separate pickup sections—one each between the E-A and D-G string pairs—with two pole pieces per string to better and more smoothly cover each string's full vibrational arc and eliminate dropouts. Wired together in series, the segmented pickup performed as a humbucker, even though each individual section was a single-coil unit.

Also in 1957 Fender changed the Precision Bass's headstock to more closely resemble that of the Stratocaster, ditching the "enlarged Tele" headstock shape.

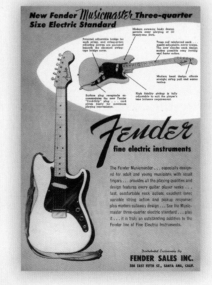

OPPOSITE TOP: *The Duo-Sonic—entirely the same as the Musicmaster, other than the inclusion of a second pickup and a three-way toggle selector.* OPPOSITE BOTTOM: *1956 Musicmaster, Fender's first student model.* THIS PAGE: *The 1955 Precision Bass featured a few design changes, most notably a contoured body and split-design pickup.*

March 28, 1961

C. L. FENDER

ELECTROMAGNETIC PICKUP FOR LUTE-TYPE MUSICAL INSTRUMENT
Filed Jan. 6, 1959

2,976,755

The Jazzmaster Cometh

The company expanded down several avenues in the 1950s, starting out primarily serving country artists, but moving confidently into the rock 'n' roll boom and then the student market. By 1957 Fender was eager to prove that its guitars could have class too.

Improvements and upgrades had been made to the Telecaster and Stratocaster, and these flagships were landing in the hands of more and more professional players. Jazz players had long been the traditionalists of the electric-guitar world: if the company could win them over too, it could finally put to rest the derision that had greeted the Broadcaster at the start of the decade and open inroads to thousands of new customers besides. The result of this effort, the Jazzmaster, became another enduring mainstay in the Fender catalog and a major favorite of several alternative genres for decades to come, though not in the jazz market that Fender had anticipated during the heated R&D process that produced it.

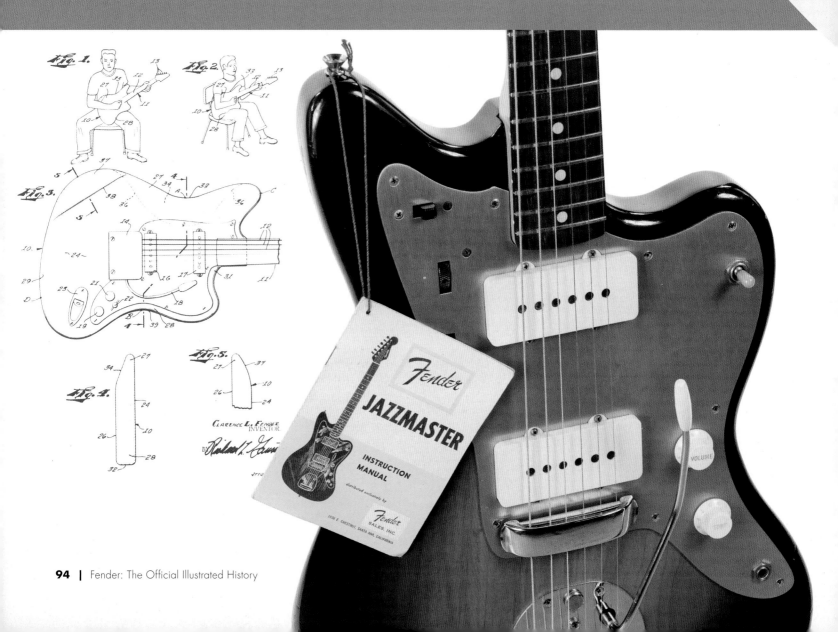

Fender's spearhead into jazz territory reasoned that the genre's traditionally minded players could be won over with a few thoughtful changes to the bolt-neck solidbody format. Many of these were touted in a 1958 ad that declared the new model "America's Finest Electric Guitar." Chief among the new features were the following:

- Entirely new, wider single-coil pickups intended to produce a warmer, rounder tone

- A new tone circuit that, in addition to a traditional "master" section that governed both pickups, offered a quick preset sound for the neck pickup alone at the flick of a switch (located on the upper horn)

- An offset-waist body design that put the guitarist's right arm in a more comfortable playing position when seated

- A new floating tremolo design partnered with a floating/rocking bridge for extremely smooth vibrato action and improved tuning stability

- A more staid, elegant-looking rosewood fingerboard and traditional Sunburst finish

The Jazzmaster displayed considerable design effort and represented an entirely new breed of Fender solidbody, boasting more complex features than any before it. The new model hit the catalog in 1958 as the brand flagship and the most expensive electric Spanish guitar Fender had to offer, retailing at $329 versus $275.50 for a '58 Stratocaster.

All that, and it failed almost entirely to catch the jazz world on fire. In theory, sure, the new neck pickup's preset rhythm tone circuit alone might have appeared a more jazz-friendly feature than anything found on another existing solidbody at the time, but aside from that there was little to grab bop, swing, or cool jazz guitarists.

OPPOSITE BOTTOM: A mint 1959 Jazzmaster, still with its hang tag, **OPPOSITE FAR LEFT:** *Jazzmaster patent drawings hint at the intended market.* **OPPOSITE TOP:** *The Jazzmaster, as featured on the cover of Fender's catalog and in period advertising.* **BELOW:** *Thumbs Carllile holds court at Fender HQ while pickin' a Jazzmaster with Fender's Freddie Tavares, (far left) and Forrest White (second from left).*

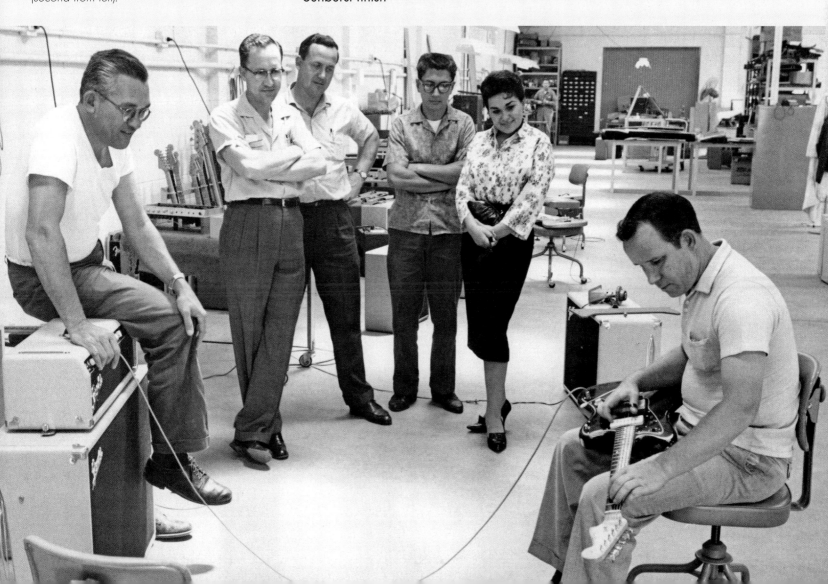

From Surf Supremo to Alternative Hero

And, on top of it all, the new Jazzmaster looked very *gadgety*—and arguably very *rock 'n' roll*.

However much of a failure the new model might have been from the perspective of the jazz market, it was a near-instant hit with the burgeoning surf-guitar scene that swelled up in California in the late 1950s and was breaking across the country by the early 1960s. The meaty-yet-twangy sound of the Jazzmaster's bridge pickup was just right for surf-guitar instrumental lead passages, the neck pickup was great for rhythm, and the smooth vibrato action beautifully suited the obligatory glissandos, dips, and vibratos intended to audibly replicate the roll and tumble of a breaking wave.

The Ventures, a Seattle band, were among the first prominent artists of the genre to put the Jazzmaster front and center, and soon it was taken up by the Astronauts, the Surfaris, the Tornadoes, and boatloads of others. The Jazzmaster also found an early proponent in Johnny

Cash guitarist Luther Perkins, neither jazz nor rock 'n' roll as such, whose use of Esquires and Telecasters had led to an association with the Fender Company. Perkins happily translated his characteristic *boom-chicka-boom-chicka* lead-rhythm style to the fancy new model.

Despite some niche-market success, however—and despite being the most expensive new guitar in the Fender catalog—the Jazzmaster's slow-burn acceptance within other genres meant it was often one of the more affordable full-sized Fender electrics on the used market in coming years. This applied even more so in the UK, where imported American guitars remained extremely expensive, especially during the faltering economy of the 1970s. If country artists were the working-class heroes of the 1950s and 1960s, punk, new wave, and indie guitarists would take on that mantle in the 1970s, 1980s, and 1990s. And the more-affordable Jazzmaster would often be their weapon of choice.

Tom Verlaine of New York band Television laced his '58 Jazzmaster all over their 1977 debut album, *Marquee Moon*, about the same time Elvis Costello posed on both front and back covers of his own debut, *My Aim Is True*, with his stripped Jazzmaster. Later on British artists Robert Smith of the Cure, Kevin Shields and Bilinda Butcher of My Bloody Valentine, Robin Guthrie of the Cocteau Twins, and, a little later, Adam Franklin of Swervedriver, Adrian Utley of Portishead, Thom Yorke of Radiohead, and a bundle of others would bend their Jazzmasters to indie and alternative hijinks. Back in the land of its birth, American noise merchants Thurston Moore and Lee Ranaldo made their Jazzmasters integral to Sonic Youth's aural assault, while J Mascis of Dinosaur Jr., Ira Kaplan of Yo La Tengo, Wayne Coyne and Steven Drozd of the Flaming Lips, and Jeff Tweedy and Nils Cline of Wilco all embraced the flagship offset.

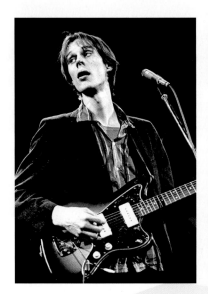  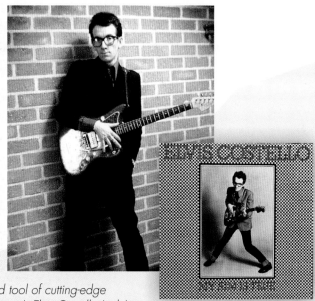

Conceived to supplant the traditional jazz box, the Jazzmaster would become a favored tool of cutting-edge rock artists like Tom Verlaine of Television (left), My Bloody Valentine's Bilinda Butcher (center), Elvis Costello (right), and J Mascis of Dinosaur Jr. (opposite).

TOP: *The Ventures were among the first surf acts to embrace the Jazzmaster.*
ABOVE: *The Jazzmaster, as featured on the cover of Fender's catalog and in period advertising.*

"I don't think of it as a tool, really. I like them as objects, more than just as a musical instrument. It's got to speak to me somehow."

J MASCIS
Interview for *Fender Feedback*:
Episode 1, March 2017

Rosewood 'Boards and Custom Colors

The Jazzmaster's rosewood fingerboard served as that elegantly rich, dark-brown slice of timber's introduction to the Fender lineup. Soon the feature proliferated to every model, so that post-1959 the integral maple fingerboard disappeared from standard Fenders until 1967. Meanwhile with Fender necks heading toward the more traditional, the bodies were soaring toward pop art with the official availability of custom color finishes.

Most accounts (including his own) indicate that George Fullerton came up with the idea for standardizing custom colors at Fender, an option that took

shape more formally around the time of the Jazzmaster's release. As Fullerton later recalled:

One day, I went down to a local paint store and I started to explain to the man what I had in mind. I had him mix some paint there on the spot and finally we came up with a red color . . . Fiesta Red! I would say probably late 1957/ early 1958. The custom colors came out about the time the Jazzmaster just came out. The reason I know that is because I had the color red put over one of the early manufactured Jazzmasters.[40]

In fact the first public mention of the availability of any alternatives to the standard Blond Telecaster and Sunburst Stratocaster came in a note at the bottom of a 1956 sales sheet that read "Stratocaster guitars are available in Du-Pont Ducco colors of the player's choice at an additional 5% cost." Prior to that, some artists had requested special colors, resulting in Bill Carson's Cimarron Red and Eldon Shamblin's gold Stratocasters.

Custom paint options had proved big sellers in the car industry in recent years, and it made sense to offer the same on electric guitars, especially as rock 'n' roll and the youth market in general were

becoming bigger consumers of the solidbodies. Paint codes from Fender's Custom Color chart, issued in 1960 and offering fifteen official colors (including Blond) in addition to the standard Sunburst, reveal their doppelgangers from the auto industry, doubling colors found on Ford's Comet, Mercury, and Lincoln models, and on GM's Chevrolet, Buick, Oldsmobile, and Cadillac models.

Custom colors became more prevalent from 1960 onward, dressing up Stratocasters and Jazzmasters most often, but occasionally daubing Telecasters and Esquires too, as well as another top-of-the-line model that was in the works for 1962.

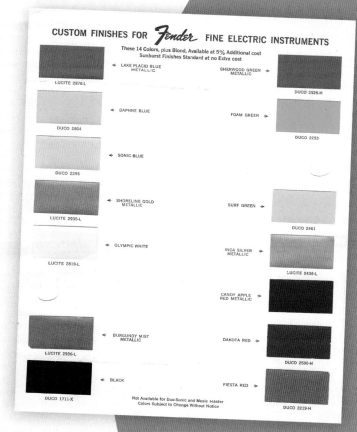

CUSTOM FINISHES FOR *Fender* FINE ELECTRIC INSTRUMENTS

These 14 Colors, plus Blond, Available at 5% Additional cost
Sunburst Finishes Standard at no Extra cost

LAKE PLACID BLUE METALLIC — LUCITE 2876-L

SHERWOOD GREEN METALLIC — DUCO 2526-H

DAPHNE BLUE — DUCO 2804

FOAM GREEN — DUCO 2253

SONIC BLUE — DUCO 2295

SHORELINE GOLD METALLIC — LUCITE 2935-L

SURF GREEN — DUCO 2461

OLYMPIC WHITE — LUCITE 2818-L

INCA SILVER METALLIC — LUCITE 2436-L

CANDY APPLE RED METALLIC

BURGUNDY MIST METALLIC — LUCITE 2936-L

DAKOTA RED — DUCO 2590-H

BLACK — DUCO 1711-X

FIESTA RED — DUCO 2219-H

Not Available for Duo-Sonic and Music Master
Colors Subject to Change Without Notice

A Jaguar Comes Out of the Jungle

With the Jazzmaster an unexpected hit on the surf scene, Fender set about developing a guitar aimed more squarely at that youthful pop and instrumental market. The result was the Jaguar, released in 1962 and different from anything the company had yet brought to show. Just before the new guitar hit the scene, though, the Bass VI of 1961 tipped off the market to Fender's thinking in the design department. With stylistic touches from the Jazzmaster, it was very much a precursor to the Jaguar and offered an extended sound for the low end.

Although the same offset-waist body shape and floating vibrato tailpiece and bridge made it a clear cousin of the Jazzmaster, the Jaguar was an even more feature-laden design—and more blinged-out too—with fancy new pickups and segmented chrome control plates for its expanded electronics. Perhaps most significantly, though, it was built to a shorter 24-inch scale length for a significantly different playing feel than any of the full-sized models that had preceded it. With all this going on, the Jaguar was also declared Fender's new top-of-the-line model, and therefore its most expensive, with a list price of $379 in Sunburst or $398 in any custom color.

Although the guitar's scale was 1½ inches shorter than that of the Telecaster, Stratocaster, and Jazzmaster, the Jaguar neck's configuration enabled the inclusion of an extra fret, making twenty-two instead of the others' twenty-one frets. Perhaps more noticeable, though, were all the gizmos and switches, and the new pickups themselves. Outwardly appearing much like the narrow single-coils on the Stratocaster, but with slightly different white plastic covers, the Jaguar pickups included a U-channel metal claw that helped both shield the coils from noise and focus their magnetic field above the poles. Otherwise they followed the traditional Fender formula, with coils wound around six individual Alnico pole pieces, much like those used on all electric Spanish models thus far.

In addition to adopting the Jazzmaster's independent preset rhythm controls for the neck pickup, the Jaguar had three slide switches on a chromed plate on the lower horn. These offered individual on/off for each pickup and instant access to a bass-cut or strangled sound, which sent the signal through a capacitor to produce a thinner, funkier sound. Finally the Jaguar's bridge included a new string mute, a hinged bracket topped with a foam-rubber pad to instantly deliver the palm-muted *plinky-plinky* sound often popular in guitar instrumentals of the day.

OPPOSITE MAIN: *The Custom Shop's Time Machine Jaguar.* **INSET AND LEFT:** *A Fender employee affixes the pickguard to a Jaguar, while Esperanza Rodriguez solders pickups circa 1958.*

The fancy new Fender was taken up by Carl Wilson of the Beach Boys and several other surf bands that also adopted the new model. Having landed as the wave was beginning to crest, however, the Jaguar found even less favor than the Jazzmaster, and it bailed out of the curl even more quickly. As such, it was subject to the same "cut-price" phenomenon that would land it in the hands of many punk, indie, and alternative players over the years.

Tom Verlaine of Television also played a Jaguar on occasion, and later the model helped fuel the grunge revolution—in both original and modified forms—as the main squeeze of Nirvana's Kurt Cobain. John Frusciante, Johnny Marr, Kevin Shields, Kurt Vile, and Adam Granduciel of the War on Drugs have all further solidified the Jaguar's alternative status.

LEFT: *Carl Wilson of the Beach Boys (front) was an early adopter of the Jaguar.*
OPPOSITE: *Former Smiths and Modest Mouse guitarist Johnny Marr wields his Jaguar.*

Chapter

7

SURF'S UP

Tolex Amps, Reverb, and Evolving Guitars

MAIN:

A Custom Shop re-creation of the Custom Telecaster. The model brought modern accoutrements to the pioneering design.

For many fans of Fender guitars and amplifiers, the transition from 1959 to 1960 is marked by the proliferation of two quite different materials: rosewood and Tolex. There's a lot more to it than that, of course, but to this day rosewood fingerboards scream "early '60s" to plenty of players and collectors. Likewise the use of the proprietary cloth-backed vinyl covering Tolex on amplifiers throughout the range signaled a significant delineation of the company's amps of the 1960s in general.

Both of these signs of a new era actually arrived just before the turn of the decade, in 1959, which was also the year Fender tried out something else a little different: versions of the Esquire and Telecaster with bound bodies, their model names appended to "Custom." Moving forward, Fender's range exploded with innovation and evolution throughout the new decade: reverb entered the amp lineup, the brand landed on effects pedals, and Fender introduced entirely new instruments before the 1960s were out—not to mention tectonic shifts at the corporate level too.

RIGHT:

Instrumental band the Astronauts display their Olympic White Jaguars, a Jazzmaster, a Jazz Bass, and blond Professional Series amps.

105

Rosewood, Binding, and 'Burst: The Telecaster Custom

The Esquire and Telecaster Custom debuted at the 1959 summer NAMM show in New York. In addition to the body binding, the new models showed off their Sunburst finishes and three-ply pickguards as standard-issue upmarket features. The latter would soon migrate to the entire guitar range, while the former often appeared in later years to have been a two-tone Sunburst due to the fading of the red color band in guitars made in the first few years of production.

These Custom variations on Fender's first solidbody, nearly ten years after its arrival, would have been a logical move for a company trying to expand its reach to more traditional players and in the wake of similar efforts with the Jazzmaster the year before. Having moved from swamp ash to alder for most Stratocasters in 1956, Fender also went with alder for the Esquire and Telecaster Custom and used it under many of the custom color Telecasters from then on. Blond Telecasters mostly continued to be made with ash bodies.

While developing the Customs, Fender had also conceived of the rosewood fingerboard as the fourth of its so-called custom appointments, but by the time the models were released, the company had decided to use the feature throughout the range. Often seen as something of an upscale move, the change might also have come directly from Leo's own desire to gain ever more respect for Fender guitars.

A 1959 Custom Esquire with body binding and rosewood fingerboard, in its original case with strap, cord, and hang tag. The '59 Custom Esquire and Telecaster brought rosewood fingerboards to Fender's seminal solidbody.

RIGHT: *A factory worker installs frets in a rosewood Jazzmaster fretboard in 1965.*
OPPOSITE: *A Stratocaster with rosewood finger-board and three-tone Sunburst finish, showing bill of sale for purchase in New York City on June 22, 1960. A view of the end of the neck reveals the "slab-board" rosewood fingerboard.*

"Interestingly, one of the reasons they went from maple to rosewood—and this is a story that I've heard (though, naturally, a lot of the stories from that day are also folklore)—was because Leo didn't like the way the finish on the necks wore out on TV," recounted former master builder Chris Fleming, now director of the Custom Shop. "They looked shabby. Back then Gibsons were considered 'real' guitars, and they all had rosewood fingerboards, so that's why Leo decided, as soon as he was able to, to start putting rosewood on the fingerboards."[41]

Another First in 1959: Tolex

Fender was still cranking out its now-legendary tweed amplifiers in 1959 and well into 1960, but before the decade's end, Leo and the team debuted two new models that presented an entirely new covering along with a new, groundbreaking design format. While running Johnny Cash's guitarist Luther Perkins through his new custom color gold Jazzmaster in June 1959, Leo also plugged the country star into a prototype of a dramatically different new amplifier.

The combo, positioned in front of Leo and Luther, is covered in what appears to be a roughly textured tan material with an unmarked, raw-metal, *forward-mounted* control panel. Controls on the two channels wear black plastic knobs of the type that would eventually be seen on the Jaguar and other 24-inch-scale guitars, and include Volume, Treble, and Bass for each of two channels, along with another two for vibrato Speed and Intensity, and finally one for Presence. The creation is widely believed to be a prototype of the new Vibrasonic model, one of Fender's first two Tolex-covered amps (alongside the Concert), as well as the first with the new forward-mounted control configuration that would soon hit the entire new brownface lineup of the early 1960s, so named for their chocolate-brown control panels.

As displayed at that summer's NAMM show and promoted in sales literature published in the latter part of 1959, this wasn't only Fender's first amplifier to incorporate the new covering and chassis/control-panel configuration: it also represented a major leap forward in amplifier design. As the sales sheet declared, "The Fender Vibrasonic Amplifier is one of the finest musical instrument amplifiers ever offered to the buying public. It offers the musician tremendous distortion-free power, plus one of the most advanced circuits in the amplifier field. . . . The over-all appearance of the Fender Vibrasonic Amp is sleek and modern in every respect and

is enhanced by the rich textured vinyl fabric covering." Dramatic claims, perhaps, but accurate, and the new configuration represented the cutting edge in guitar amplification.

At the time of its debut, the Vibrasonic was far and away Fender's most expensive amplifier, at a list price of $479. Consider that the high-powered tweed Twin of 1958–1960, which delivered 80 watts through two 12-inch Jensen Alnico speakers, was the next priciest at $399 that same year—despite offering double the Vibrasonic's output through two speakers—and that's quite a leap. That said, the new Tolex combo did also include Fender's lush new harmonic vibrato effect, while also sporting an extremely expensive 15-inch JBL D-130 speaker.

It's unclear whether any Vibrasonic combos actually shipped before early January 1960, by which time Fender was also promoting the second of its new Tolex-covered combos, the 4×10-inch Concert, which was similarly equipped with the dramatic new vibrato. The earliest of these amps were covered in a rough, pinkish-brown Tolex that would be changed in favor of a more consistently light-brown/tan Tolex later that year as the entire Fender range—other than the wee Champ—morphed and shifted to front-mounted configurations.

OPPOSITE: *Leo Fender sits on the desk in his R&D lab in 1959, while Luther Perkins plays a Jazzmaster through a prototype of the forthcoming Vibrasonic amplifier.* RIGHT: *An early 1960 Vibrasonic in rough pinkish-brown Tolex, with rare "center-volume" positioning and tweed-era grille cloth. The top-of-the-line Vibrasonic used an expensive 15-inch JBL D130 speaker.*

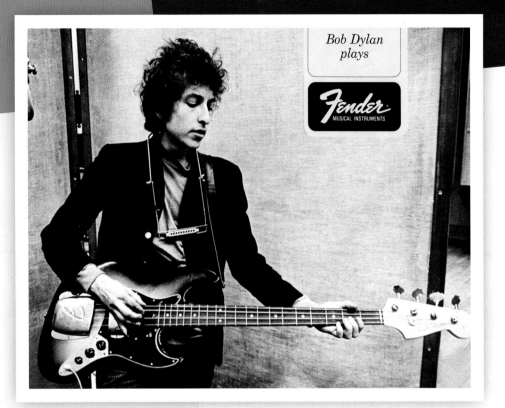

The Jazz Bass: A Deluxe Four-String

Also in 1960 Fender delivered a new full-scale bass guitar briefly known as the Deluxe Model, before a name change to Jazz Bass more fully stated its intentions. The new model's body was shaped much like an enlarged Jazzmaster, with an offset-waist design. As with the Jazzmaster, Fender hoped its narrower, rounder neck shape would appeal to jazz players.

OPPOSITE TOP: Bob Dylan was famously photographed plucking a Jazz Bass during studio sessions in 1965. OPPOSITE: A 1960 Jazz Bass with its original rough-brown Tolex case leans on a tweed 1960 Bassman 4x10 combo, Fender's bass amp at the time of the new four-string's arrival. THIS PAGE: The concentric volume and tone knobs on a 1960 Jazz Bass.

Prototypes made in 1959 initially carried wide single-coil pickups that looked much like reworked versions of Jazzmaster pickups, but upon its release the Jazz Bass was equipped with two narrow single-coil pickups with eight pole pieces each, one positioned approximately halfway between bridge and neck, and the other much nearer the bridge. Initially, controls included individual concentric Volume and Tone pots for each pickup, a configuration later changed to individual Volume controls and a shared Tone control.

Between the pickups and the available controls, the Jazz Bass offered a lot of sonic versatility, delivering warm, full tones from the neck pickup; bright, punchy snarl from the bridge pickup; or a blend of these voices by combining both pickups as desired. Since the introduction of the Jazz Bass, the Precision Bass has often been considered Fender's bass for rockers. While it has indeed won over a lot of jazz players, the Jazz Bass has also been taken up by musicians playing just about every style of amplified music. From virtuoso Jaco Pastorius, funk rocker Flea, and R&B star Verdine White, to rock pioneers Noel Redding and Geddy Lee, the Jazz Bass has proved its flexibility time and again.

Meanwhile, as Fender's amp lineup evolved dramatically in the early 1960s, the basses received a proper amp to help them stand out on their own. The last comprehensive range of tweed models had appeared in 1959 and early 1960, and the Bassman remained a 4×10-inch tweed combo for the 1960 model year. By 1961, though, Fender's full amplifier line had evolved so much that looked like it came from an entirely different company.

Numerous influential players have taken up the Jazz Bass. Earth, Wind & Fire's Verdine White (left), the late virtuoso Jaco Pastorius (opposite top left), Geddy Lee of Rush (opposite top right), and Red Hot Chili Pepper Flea (opposite bottom).

MAIN: *Surf guitar legend Dick Dale (fourth from right) and the Del-Tones famously employed a hot-rodded Showman with a Reverb unit.* **INSET:** *A 1961 Showman head and Tone Ring 1×15 speaker cabinet.* **OPPOSITE LEFT:** *The Bassman migrated into the piggyback format in the early '60s. It had evolved to blackface cosmetics by the time this 1964 example was made.* **OPPOSITE RIGHT:** *A blond 1962 Bandmaster from the Professional Series.*

The Showman Goes On and Professional Piggybacks Follow

Stand a late tweed Bassman beside an early Showman—both amps available simultaneously for a brief period in 1960—and the differences between them are dramatic, to say the least. Fender hit its stride quickly in the new decade, rapidly setting new standards for amplification, some of which aimed to address guitarists' ever-increasing need for volume as rock and pop took to bigger and bigger stages.

Pioneering surf guitarist Dick Dale made as strong a case as anyone for more power. Nearly every weekend, Dale pummeled his Stratocaster through Fender amps in front of his band, the Del-Tones, before crowds of two to three thousand stomping surfer teens at the Rendezvous Ballroom in Balboa, California. He found the existing rigs inadequate for re-creating the roil and tumble of the surf experience, so he let

Leo Fender know about it. The Showman was Fender's reply: a big amp for big shows in an era when rock 'n' roll was clearly here to stay.

The first configuration of the Showman had the four 5881 output tubes (a.k.a. 6L6s) of the Twin, with the preamp stages and output transformer of the Vibrasonic. The amp "head" or "top" ran into a separate extension cabinet carrying a single 12- or 15-inch JBL speaker mounted to a "tone ring," a complex ported, dual-baffle configuration that enabled a fuller, more hi-fi-like speaker response. In theory this power stage might have delivered 80 to 100 watts, but the output transformer was likely holding back its potential. The single speaker would have had trouble handling that wattage at full blast anyway. In 1961 Fender introduced a larger output transformer to the

Showman, and in 1962 the company offered the option of a 2×15-inch cabinet (minus the complex ported tone-ring baffles) as the Dual Showman, an amp finally capable of handling the maelstrom from what was now 85 to 100 watts of power.

In Fender's 1961 catalog new Bandmaster, Bassman, and Tremolux models had taken on piggyback (a.k.a. stack) configurations in Fender's Professional Amplifiers lineup. All were covered in a blond Tolex with oxblood grille cloth, a look that was also given to the Twin combo. All other combos retained light-brown Tolex.

Also in light-brown Tolex and prototyped in 1961 was an entirely new Fender product. Neither amplifier nor guitar, it hit the scene in 1962 as a link between the two with the intention of further defining the sound of surf music.

Reverb Lands with a Splash

The Fender Reverb Unit appeared in the 1961 catalog, becoming more properly available in 1962, when players by the score took up the new effect for use with vocals and guitar alike. Often considered one of the best-sounding forms this effect has ever taken, the Reverb Unit used two preamp tubes and a 6K6GT output tube (for which a similar 6V6GT was substituted in later reissue units) to drive a long-spring reverb pan. The unit's Tone, Mix, and Dwell controls enabled the player to blend its lush, watery, echoey sound with the guitar's dry signal as desired and send it on to a conventional amplifier.

Given the configuration of guitar amps of the day, and their lack of effects loops, the Reverb Unit was designed to be used between guitar and amp, into the main input, rather than farther along in the signal chain, where reverb is more often found today (and where Fender also would soon put it).

OPPOSITE: *The front and top control panel of a 1963 Reverb Unit in brown Tolex.* ABOVE: *A 1962 Reverb Unit sits atop a 1962 Concert amplifier.* ABOVE RIGHT: *Stevie Ray Vaughan flips out in front of his mid-60s 1×15 Vibroverb.* RIGHT: *The short-lived Vibroverb, Fender's first production amplifier with built-in reverb.*

Developed late in 1962 and available in early 1963, the Vibroverb was a 2×10-inch combo with the size and power of the existing Super, but now included a built-in tube-driven spring reverb governed by a single Reverb knob along with bias-modulated tremolo. A rare find on today's collector's market, the Vibroverb experienced one of the shortest production runs of any Fender amp of such significance. As groundbreaking as this combo might have been, it was also rapidly superseded by a growing lineup of reverb-equipped amps, as Fender added the effect to new and existing models later that same year.

Late 1963 saw the arrival of the Deluxe Reverb, Super Reverb, and Twin Reverb combos, the latter prototyped in early '63 according to one existing example. All were now in new businesslike black Tolex coverings with silver grille cloth and black control panels (hence the term blackface associated with them). They marked yet another era of Fender amps seemingly rushing in on the heels of a brownface era that had barely gotten started. In 1964, the 2×10-inch Vibrolux Reverb and 1×10-inch Princeton Reverb joined the team, and the by the end of that year the Champ had finally morphed out of its narrow-panel cabinet and into a new rendition of the blackface styling. The Vibro-Champ version offered built-in tremolo.

THIS PAGE: *This early-1963 Twin Reverb prototype was given by Leo Fender to the late pedal-steel player and inventor Red Rhodes, who used it in the studio for many years before it was lost in storage. It is housed in a brown Tolex cabinet that was carefully painted black. Inside, Vibroverb preamp meets harmonic vibrato and a blond-Twin output stage—all via eight preamp tubes.* **OPPOSITE MAIN:** *A 1962 Vibrolux in smooth-brown Tolex.* **OPPOSITE INSET:** *Fender's 1963–65 catalog cover featured the new flagship combo, the Twin Reverb.*

Desert-Island Amps

By the mid-1960s the full blackface Fender lineup was widely recognized as the finest and most professional range of guitar amplifiers of the day, while also establishing the sound of tube-driven spring reverb that would remain that effect's benchmark for decades to come. It's no exaggeration to say every member of Fender's reverb-carrying amp family circa 1964 retains legendary status today and has become iconic in the pantheon of tone, while several amps that lacked it—the Bassman, for one—are almost equally admired for their own capabilities.

For their combination of stellar tone, portability, and versatile features, smaller members of the family, like the Deluxe Reverb and Princeton Reverb, have become many players' idea of the ultimate desert-island amp, while also being classic grab 'n' go club and studio amps.

The blackface sound itself is a tonal archetype that has reached far beyond the bounds of Fender products. It can be described as clear, crisp, and articulate, yet offering very playable dynamics and an appealing breakup when distortion sets in, the blackface sonic template is also defined by a slightly scooped (a.k.a. midrange-recessed) voicing, with firm lows and somewhat glassy, sparkling highs. These characteristics make the 1963–1967 amps go-tos for twangy country or jangly West Coast guitar styles, but also suit stinging, biting blues and driving rock 'n' roll when cranked up a little. Interestingly the blackface amps delivered a sound quite

different from the more mid-forward response, somewhat softer lows, and creamier highs of the tweed combos of the 1950s—yet both remain archetypal templates of the Fender tone.

Through the years, Muddy Waters, Wes Montgomery, Michael Bloomfield, Roy Buchanan, Danny Gatton, Stevie Ray Vaughan, Robert Cray, Ronnie Earl, Derek Trucks, Pete Anderson, Alex Chilton, Jim Campilongo, Michael Landau, Lee Ranaldo, Johnny Marr, Tom Verlaine, and Richard Lloyd— among a gazillion others—have plied their trade with Fender blackface amplifiers.

OPPOSITE: *Muddy Waters plays his iconic red Telecaster through a Fender Reverb combo.*
ABOVE: *The dual blackface Deluxe Reverb combos in Richard Thompson's stage rig.*

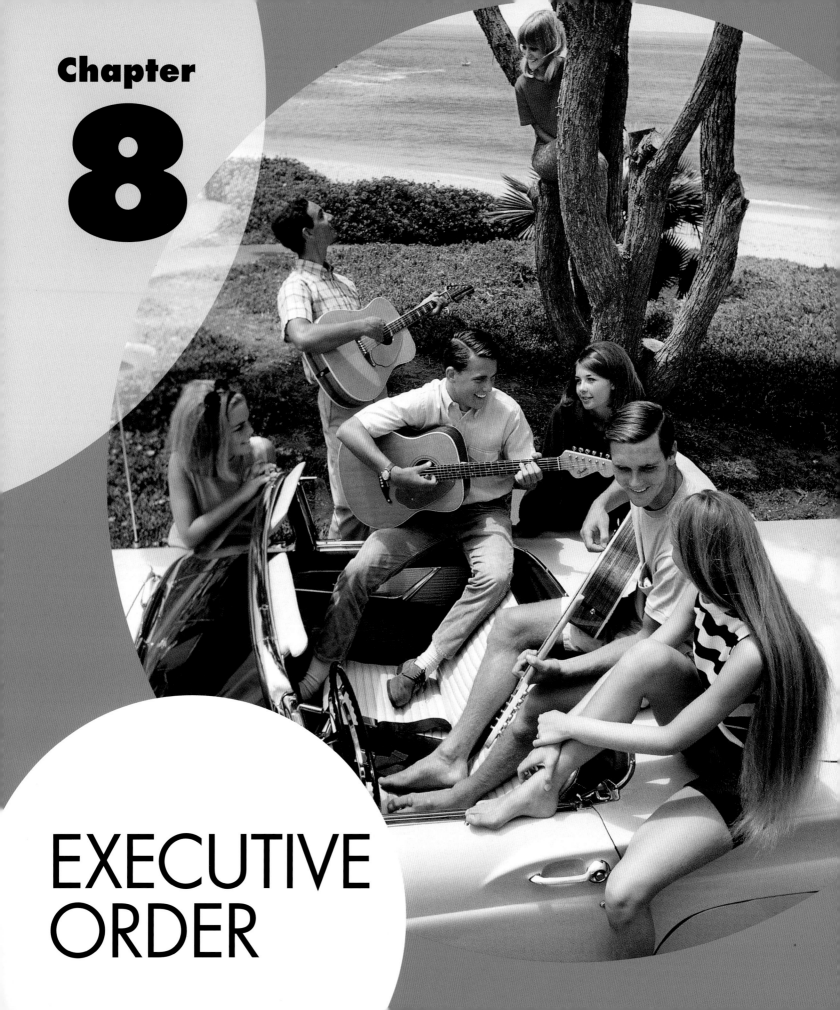

Chapter

8

EXECUTIVE ORDER

The Mustang Debuts and CBS Comes Knocking

The 1960s were a time of tumultuous change at Fender. One of the most notable changes of ownership in the company's history took place in the middle of the decade. At the start of that era, though, Fender was going from strength to strength, showing no indication of slowing its roll.

By the start of the new decade, Fender was well past the early doubters who had denigrated the first production solidbody electric guitar and was firmly established as one of the most revolutionary, and most successful, players in the field of musical instrument manufacturing. As such, Leo and Don were looking to expand the product base, introducing new instruments that might have seemed anathema to the Fender brand just a few years before.

Leo decided the time was right to introduce a Fender line of acoustic guitars. In 1962 he hired former Rickenbacker employee Roger Rossmeisl, trained as a luthier in his native Germany, to help with the venture. The result was a relatively traditional flat-top acoustic guitar, but one made with a screwed-on neck and the iconic Fender six-a-side headstock, plus an unusual reinforcing tube running inside the body between the tail block and neck block to help maintain stability over time.

Debuted at the Chicago NAMM show in the summer of 1963, the full acoustic lineup included the King (later renamed Kingman), Concert, Classic, and Folk (soon deleted), all of which went into full production soon after at Fender's main facility. Shortly thereafter a dedicated acoustic guitar factory was built in Anaheim, California, where the line would be expanded in another few years to include the more affordable Malibu and Newporter models and the twelve-string Shenandoah and Villager.

Although the original line of US-made Fender acoustics lasted only until the end of the decade, they made quite a splash while they were available: Elvis Presley, Buck Owens, Johnny Cash, Ray Davies, and several others all played Fender flat-tops at one time or another.

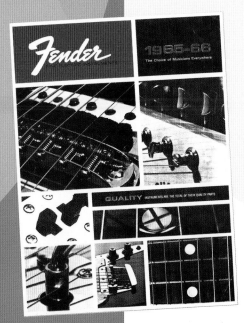

Ray Davies of the Kinks was one high-profile artist who played a Fender flat-top.

125

ABOVE: *Fender Mustang in Dakota Red with the spiffy "Competition Stripe."*
OPPOSITE: *Mustang bass in Fiesta Red.*

Mustang Runs Free and Student Models Evolve

In August 1964 Fender introduced another classic in the making, the Mustang. Initially available with either a 24- or 22.5-inch scale length, the Mustang was the new flagship of a revamped student lineup that also included the Musicmaster II and Duo-Sonic II.

The Mustang's body was similar to that of the Musicmaster and Duo-Sonic that preceded it but was gently reshaped, with a slightly offset waist and a subtly different look for the horns and cutaways. Most notably, perhaps, the Mustang sported a new breed of Fender vibrato (making this the third type of vibrato used

on the company's four vibrato-carrying guitars thus far), along with two three-way slide switches for its two pickups. In addition to on/off duties that enabled selection of either pickup individually or both used in parallel (the traditional middle-position sound), these switches allowed for an out-of-phase selection that yielded a thinner, funkier tone.

At the time of the Mustang's release, its siblings received the same body and neck updates, scale options, and switching configuration (in the case of the fellow two-pickup model) in their new guises as the Musicmaster II and Duo-Sonic II. These two nonvibrato models

were also given new bridges configured on larger, semitrapezoidal plates, which looked less like the chopped-down Telecaster bridges of their predecessors.

All three guitars were now available in three nifty new finish options too: red, white, and blue. While today these are often referred to as Dakota Red, Olympic White, and Daphne Blue—after the options from the custom color chart they most closely resemble—their proper names were the simple old chromatic monikers. Given its similarity to the Mustang and lack of a vibrato feature, the Duo-Sonic II was discontinued after 1969.

By this time the Mustang was sporting its spiffy new "Competition Stripe" cosmetic treatment: a racing stripe that dashed diagonally across the bass-side lower bout to adorn a number of new finish options. In 1966, Fender also introduced the Mustang Bass. This was the company's first shorter, student-model bass, built to a 30-inch scale length. It was equipped with a single split-coil pickup, much like a smaller version of that on the Precision Bass, but with its pole pieces fully encased beneath plastic covers.

Despite their student model status, Duo-Sonics and Mustangs have landed in the hands of dozens of influential artists over the years. Rory Gallagher, John McLaughlin, Jimi Hendrix, David Byrne, Todd Rundgren, Adrian Belew, and Kurt Cobain all made groundbreaking music on these shorter-scale Fenders. They continue to appeal to contemporary artists like beabadoobee, Lindsey Jordan of Snail Mail, Matthew Healey of the 1975, and Brendon Urie of Panic at the Disco.

While Kurt Cobain (center) was arguably the highest-profile Mustang player, the guitars and basses have gained favor with modern artists such as beabadoobee (left) and the Regrettes (right).

Executive Action

By 1964 Fender employed approximately five hundred workers in a complex that spanned twenty-seven buildings in Fullerton. The guitar industry was booming, business was good, and Fender was right at the center of it—but Leo Fender himself was feeling run down and was no longer really up to running the company. From one groundbreaking development to another, Leo had been burning the midnight oil since the mid-1940s. He was perpetually driven to invent new and better tools for the guitarists who had made the Fender name famous, but he had never had much of an interest in running a business. And as the middle of the decade approached, Fender was a *big* business.

On top of all that, Leo had been fighting a strep infection contracted in the mid-1950s. His sinuses were continually aggravated, leaving him even more exhausted than he might already have been at the helm of a guitar-and-amp maker that had grown exponentially for a full two decades. It was clear to Don Randall from discussions with his partner that Leo was simply tired of the effort, and through the early part of 1964 the pair discussed selling the company.

Randall recalled the conversation many years later: "[Leo] said, 'Well, Don, I think I ought to get a million and a half dollars now,'" to which Randall replied, "Well, that's probably not too far off. . . . Why don't I go ahead and see what I can do with the companies?"[42]

Randall spoke to Merrill Lynch about going public, which Leo said he didn't want to do, instead kicking off early assessments and negotiations for the Baldwin Piano Company to purchase Fender. Ultimately unhappy with Baldwin's terms, Randall began speaking with one of the country's biggest broadcasting corporations, following an introduction by Merrill Lynch. It was this lead that began to look more and more promising.

BELOW LEFT: *Don Randall as photographed by Robert Perine in the mid-60s.* BELOW RIGHT: *Leo Fender in his office, as photographed by Robert Perine.*

CBS Comes Calling

In the mid-1960s Columbia Broadcasting System Inc. (CBS) was a large radio and television broadcasting corporation looking to diversify its financial interests; in particular, it was looking for a foothold in the musical instrument industry. At the time, CBS was home to hit TV series such as *The Ed Sullivan Show*, *The Andy Griffith Show*, and *The Beverly Hillbillies*, and the results of the negotiations tell us that it had some money to spend.

After plenty of back-and-forth, Randall hammered out a deal for CBS to purchase both the Fender Electric Instrument Co. and Fender Sales for a whopping $13 million, the highest price paid to date for the purchase of a musical instrument company (and, it's worth noting, nearly $2 million more than they had paid for the New York Yankees baseball team just the year before). The fine print was agreed to at the end of 1964 and the sale was finalized on January 5, 1965.

ABOVE: *After the sale, Forrest White transitioned to the position of plant manager.* **RIGHT:** *The letter confirming the sale of Fender to CBS in late 1964.* **BELOW:** *CBS paid $2 million more for Fender than they did for the New York Yankees just the year before.* **OPPOSITE:** *Leo used a portion of his proceeds from the sale to buy an oceangoing boat. He's seen here in Hawaii and in a marina with George Fullerton (left) and Forrest White (right).*

December 28, 1964

Columbia Records Distribution Corp.
799 Seventh Avenue
New York, New York

Attention: Mr. Clive J. Davis, Secretary

Dear Sirs:

Pursuant to Article First C. I of the Agreement dated December 15, 1964, between Donald D. Randall, Jean E. Randall, C. Leo Fender and Esther M. Fender, as Sellers, and you, as Purchaser, it is hereby requested, on behalf of the Sellers, that two certified or bank cashier's checks be delivered at the Closing, of which one shall be payable to the order of C. Leo Fender and Esther M. Fender, in the amount of $5,735,000, and the other shall be payable to the order of Donald D. Randall and Jean E. Randall, in the amount of $5,265,000.

Very truly yours,

Donald D. Randall

Jean E. Randall

C. Leo Fender

Esther M. Fender

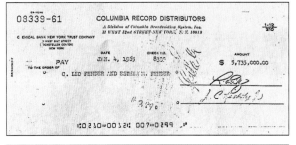

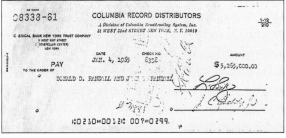

CBS changed the company name to Fender Musical Instruments, making it a division of another of its arms in the entertainment industry, the Columbia Records Distribution Corp. Randall was named vice president and general manager, the latter ceding to him the position to which Forrest White had been promoted, while White was moved back to the job of plant manager. Bill Carson made the transfer to CBS and moved to Fender Sales in 1967. George Fullerton and Freddie Tavares also made the transition, although Dale Hyatt departed the company. Leo Fender was retained as a consultant in research and development for five years, and Randall also signed a five-year employment contract with CBS, both with ten-year noncompete clauses intended to prevent them from setting up companies in the musical instrument business independent of the CBS-owned Fender company.

Leo used a portion of his own proceeds from the sale to buy a large oceangoing boat, which he and Esther frequently took between the mainland and Catalina Island. Other than that, he appears to have spent very little time in the factory, while Randall busied himself with the demands of his position, traveling frequently between the California facility and his corporate office in the CBS building in New York.

Forrest White later recalled Leo's departure as owner of the company that still bore his name:

Monday evening, January 4, 1965, I went down to see Leo in his lab for the last time. We both found it difficult to act nonchalant. I helped him carry his personal belongings out to his car, pretended not to notice the tears in his eyes, hoped he hadn't noticed mine. He got into his car and I walked to the side gate. He stopped briefly on his way out, paused and said, "I don't know what I would have done without you." . . . He stepped on the gas and was out the gate before I could answer. That was the last time I would let him out the gate as I had done so many times before. I watched until his car was out of sight.[43]

Several disparate reports indicate that Leo Fender might have been led to believe that his medical condition, aggravating though it might have been, was even more serious than it was, possibly even life-threatening. After suffering the affliction for nearly two decades, however, and selling his company in part as a means of reducing the mounting stress and exhaustion, he started treatments with a new doctor. "About 1968, I found a doctor who knew the appropriate treatment for the infection," he later told *Guitar Player*, "and I haven't been bothered with it since."[44]

Changes Creeping In

As with any big company seeking a major investment, CBS obviously bought Fender to make a profit. Even though the former Fender Electric Instrument Co. had become extremely successful and very profitable, CBS gradually introduced cost-cutting and efficiency measures that its executives believed would better pad out the profit margin. Some, however, eventually damaged the reputations of the guitars and amplifiers with players.

This situation also help established the most significant delineation in the history of Fender production: pre-CBS vs. post-CBS. Forever after, the former tag has denoted the most highly desirable era of Fender guitars and amplifiers for players and collectors alike, a contrast seen most keenly a decade after the sale, when the quality of the instruments and amplifiers produced was widely perceived to have declined.

Through the remainder of the 1960s, Fender by and large maintained excellent quality throughout the range. Most players have come to recognize that, for example, a 1966 or 1967 Stratocaster, Telecaster, Jazzmaster, Deluxe Reverb, or Bassman made under CBS's ownership will generally perform just as well as one made a year or two before the purchase. Certain changes did begin to creep in, however, many of which—in hindsight—appear to have been wrought upon classic products by executives with relatively little understanding of the finer points of manufacturing high-quality musical instruments.

The following first changes were largely cosmetic, but others are widely thought to have detracted from the overall quality of the guitars that received them.

- Logos. The Stratocaster and Jazzmaster had already received a thicker gold logo with black outline (often called a transition logo), designed by Robert Perine, in the summer of 1964; the Telecaster retained its original thin spaghetti logo for about another year. In 1967 all Fender guitars received the new CBS-era logo, with bold black letters and a thin gold outline.

- Headstocks. All guitars other than the Telecaster received a bigger headstock at the end of 1965, which better displayed the Fender logo. The standard Telecaster model would forever retain its original slender, rolling headstock shape.

OFFICIAL FENDER TRADEMARK
To standardize on the appearance of all products and packaging and to coordinate advertising, literature and sales promotion, the trademark uses shown on this sheet have been adopted.

FOR PRODUCT NAMEPLATES AND DECALS.

FOR DISPLAYS, SIGNS, PACKAGING AND LABELS.

FOR ADVERTISING AND SALES PROMOTION.

OPPOSITE: *Robert Perine photos depict the Fender facilities in 1966, after the sale to CBS.* **ABOVE:** *1966 Stratocaster in three-tone Sunburst.* **ABOVE LEFT:** *The post-sale period saw a reimagining of the iconic Fender logo.* **LEFT:** *Perhaps the most noted change of the CBS era: all guitars other than the Telecaster received a bigger headstock to better display the Fender logo.*

- Maple fingerboard option. Fender reintroduced an optional maple fingerboard in 1967, although these were constructed in the same way as necks with rosewood fingerboards: routing the maple neck blank for the truss rod, then gluing a maple cap fingerboard over the top of it (hence the absence of the walnut skunk stripe on the back, or the teardrop above the nut).

- F-logo tuners. Also in 1967, Fender stopped buying in Kluson tuners and instead commissioned its own from Schaller. Stamped with an "F" on the back of the enclosures, these often didn't hold up as well over the years as the older Klusons.

- Finishes. In 1968 Fender dispensed with its traditional nitrocellulose lacquer finishes and began spraying guitars with thick, plasticky, polyester finishes. The change was likely introduced to simultaneously make the finishing process easier and to produce harder, longer-wearing finishes (thus reducing warranty issues). These poly finishes are widely believed to have dampened the resonance of the guitars that received them, choking their tone as a result; many guitarists claim the poly-finished necks don't feel as good in the hand as those finished in nitro.

The brochure accompanying this
1966 CBS Stratocaster detailed
here enumerates the guitar's features.

Although the large headstock is often viewed as a feature that distinguishes the post-CBS Stratocasters and their siblings from those that came before, the early large-head models are considered very much the equivalent of the late pre-CBS and transition-era Strats. More detrimental changes to the Stratocaster, however, were just around the corner in the new decade, waiting to take it further from the template that made pre-CBS examples legendary.

Fender had a rocky stretch of road ahead in many regards, to be sure, although several adaptations under CBS introduced beloved new renditions of classic models. And the remainder of the 1960s still had some groovy alternative new models to deliver too.

The Robert Perine beach girl campaign of the mid-'60s wisely attracted the growing youth demographic.

More Robert Perine ad photography of the period. "Banjo girl" was Perine's daughter, Jorlie. Her circle of friends was often enlisted as ad models.

Chapter
9

FEELIN'
GROOVY

Pianos, Pedals, and Psychedelic Guitars

Fender as a corporation—and many of its products—exited the 1960s in quite different shape than how they had entered the decade. It was a decade of major growth and change: while several new products had been added during this time, the full-steam-ahead drive for progress would result in some wrong turns as the company plowed into the 1970s under CBS ownership. Meanwhile the company's expansion into other musical instrument markets delivered some genuine classics—along with a few clunkers.

MAIN:
Two models with a Coronado in a Robert Perine advertising photo shoot.

RIGHT:
A "Fender lovin' care" button from 1969.

The Fender Rhodes Piano

Fender's production of its iconic analog keyboard instrument came courtesy of Harold Rhodes, a Californian who had founded and managed a chain of piano schools as a young man in the 1930s before joining the Army Air Corps in World War II. While seeking therapeutic recreation for wounded soldiers during his downtime, Rhodes discovered that aluminum pipes from the wings of B-17 bombers sounded surprisingly good when cut to specific lengths to produce precise notes. The seeds for an entirely new form of compact piano were sown.

After the war, Rhodes manufactured his own version of the piano for several years before entering an agreement with Fender in 1959. Leo, in fact, disliked the sound produced by the upper register of the Rhodes Piano, but felt the lower register worked well as an alternative bass instrument. The resulting Fender Rhodes Piano Bass offered thirty-two keys from the bass register of the traditional piano in a compact casing, giving bass-less bands a convenient way to fill in the low end. By this time, Rhodes's piano included an electromagnetic pickup system to produce an electrical signal from the vibration of the iron tone bars struck by the action of the instrument's keys (Rhodes had moved on from aluminum aircraft tubes), and Fender cased up the instrument in a Tolex-covered box with a fiberglass top made by a local boat manufacturer.

Although it was no huge success, the Fender Rhodes Piano Bass proved popular with several working bands. And, whether we know it or not, we have all heard the instrument in action: with no bassist in the band, the Doors' keyboardist Ray Manzarek perched a Fender Rhodes Piano Bass on top of his Vox Continental organ to play the bass parts for live performances and many recordings.

In 1965 shortly after CBS's purchase of Fender, Don Randall approached Harold Rhodes about producing a full version of his piano, and a new deal was struck. The Fender Rhodes Electric Piano was first released as a seventy-three-key instrument, appearing much like an extended version of the Piano Bass but constructed as a Suitcase model with a built-in 50-watt amplifier. In 1970 Fender introduced the Stage Model—available without an amplifier attached—as well as an eighty-eight-key version in both Stage and Suitcase versions.

Although it doesn't sound much like a traditional acoustic piano, the Fender Rhodes introduced an appealing new sound to popular music. Its mellow, rich, expressive tone seemed tailor made for jazz, although that rather staid genre was somewhat slow on the uptake.

Upon arriving to the first sessions for Miles Davis's 1968 album *Miles in the Sky*, piano prodigy Herbie Hancock was puzzled by the lack of an acoustic piano in Columbia Studio B in New York City, until Davis—ever the sonic pioneer—pointed him toward the Fender Rhodes Electric Piano in the corner. "You want me to play that toy?" Hancock replied. But play he did, laying down the first examples of a sound that became central to his compelling marriage of jazz, funk, electro, and classical in years to come.[45]

Jazz great Bill Evans began incorporating the Rhodes into his sound in the early 1970s, often setting one up on stage alongside his acoustic grand piano, even including the instrument's name in the full title of his 1970 album, *From Left to Right: Playing the Fender-Rhodes Electric Piano and the Steinway Piano*. Over the years, Oscar Peterson, George Duke, Ray Charles, the Beatles, Stevie Wonder, Elton John, Billy Joel, and a host of others employed the Fender Rhodes Piano's mellow, emotive sound when the mood called for it.

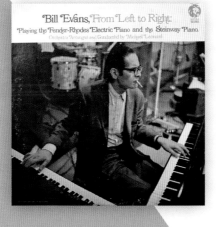

TOP: *Ray Manzarek, John Densmore, and Jim Morrison gather over a Rhodes Piano Bass as the Doors prepare for a concert in Frankfurt, Germany, in September 1968.* **ABOVE:** *A Rhodes Piano Bass and several guitars help Fender woo younger customers at a "Teenage Fair" in 1963.* **FAR LEFT:** *A 73-key Rhodes Stage Model Electric Piano.* **LEFT:** *Jazz great Bill Evans elevated the status of the Rhodes Electric Piano by playing it alongside his Steinway grand.*

Chasing the Beatles: Twelve-Strings and Hollowbody Electrics

Following their appearance on *The Ed Sullivan Show* on February 9, 1964, the massive popularity of the Beatles—and of British Invasion artists in general—left most musical instrument manufacturers chasing the Fab Four's preferred gear in a bid to lure hundreds of thousands of fans to their brands. Fender was no different, and while the company's instruments and amplifiers didn't feature heavily in the band's lineup in the mid-1960s (although John Lennon had prominently used a tweed Deluxe combo in the early years), there was still good commercial sense in tracking the Mop Tops' popularity.

One trend was seen in the thinline hollowbody electric Epiphone and Gretsch models that the Beatles played at one time or another, a style that Fender landed for itself with help from Roger Rossmeisl, the developer of the company's flat-top acoustic line earlier in the decade. Designed and announced in 1965, and more widely available from 1966 onward, the resultant Coronado lineup offered fully hollow, thinline, double-cutaway electric guitars that used single-coil DeArmond pickups (one or two on the I and II models respectively) and the option of a fixed trapeze tailpiece or one mounted with a vibrato that functioned similarly to those used on the Mustang.

ABOVE LEFT: *Freddie Tavares checks a newly minted Coronado.*
ABOVE RIGHT: *Roger Rossmeisl, pioneer of Fender acoustic and semiacoustic guitar designs, at the factory in the early '60s.*
OPPOSITE TOP LEFT: *Spraying Coronado bodies at the Fender factory.*
OPPOSITE TOP RIGHT: *Fender employees construct pickup bobbins in the mid-60s.* **OPPOSITE BOTTOM:** *Elvis Presley and Nancy Sinatra with a Coronado II in the 1968 movie Speedway.*

Coronado Bass I and Bass II models followed shortly after the guitars, and Fender delivered a Coronado XII electric twelve-string in 1967. That year also saw the release of the hippie-tinged Coronado-based Fender Wildwood series, guitars made from laminated beech wood stained by injecting the fast-growing trees with colored dyes, which produced random patterns in the wood when it was milled and laminated (an option also applied to Fender's Kingman flat-top guitars at the time).

Despite its bolt-on neck and familiar six-a-side headstock, the Coronado was a rather "un-Fender-like" model in other regards, although it did earn cult-like popularity among many players. Sonically adventurous Coronado players of later years included Jack White of the White Stripes, Stuart Braithwaite of Mogwai, and both Colin Greenwood and Thom Yorke of Radiohead (taking up the Coronado Bass this time). But the just-for-show example that likely earned greatest exposure involved Elvis Presley's miming of the solo to "There Ain't Nothing Like a Song" in the 1968 movie *Speedway*, in which he briefly strums, then thumps upon, a tasty Sunburst Coronado II, while the band on stage behind him play a Stratocaster, a Precision Bass, and another new guitar-boom-inspired offering: the Fender Electric XII.

Introduced around the same time as the Coronado, also in the wake of the immensely popular Rickenbacker 360/12, the Electric XII had an off-set-waist body similar to the Jazzmaster and Jaguar, a bridge adapted from the Duo-Sonic II design, and two split-single-coil pickups that followed in the footsteps of the revised Precision Bass units. Its four-way rotary switch offered an out-of-phase selection in addition to the traditional neck, bridge, and middle. One of its most notable characteristics, however, was the hockey-stick head-stock, which had a Gumby-like protuber-ance jutting downward from the end of its double-six-a-side construction.

With just a couple years left in the electric twelve-string craze at the time of its arrival, the Electric XII never rose to first-rank collectability status, although it was used by several prominent artists in the early years, particularly in the studio. Pete Townshend used an Electric XII on "Sparks" and "Undertore" for the Who's 1969 rock opera *Tommy*, and in 1970 Jimmy Page laid down one of the most famous electric twelve-string recordings of all time, playing the haunting introduction to "Stairway to Heaven" on this Fender.

You won't part with yours either.

Wherever you go, you'll find Fender!
*For your personal selection see the complete line of Fender Fine Electric Instruments (like the sensational new "Electric Twelve" guitar shown above) on display at leading music dealers throughout the world.

Fender
SALES, INC.

SANTA ANA, CALIFORNIA

OPPOSITE: *A 1965 Electric XII with original literature, hang tag, spare strings, and polishing cloth.* ABOVE: *A model displays an Electric XII in one of Fender's reoccurring mid-60s beach-themed photo shoots.* LEFT: *The Electric XII gets Perine's advertising treatment.*

Fender Effects Go Psychedelic

Effects units were nothing new to Fender, although they'd rarely been central to the lineup. The company had briefly marketed an EccoFonic tape-loop echo unit in 1958–1959 that was produced by an outside manufacturer, and then introduced its own solid-state tape echo in 1963, which never gained much traction. The Fender Reverb Unit of 1961 was an undeniable classic, however, and in 1967 it was joined by Fender's biggest effects unit of all time—in the physical sense, at least.

The Vibratone was a rotating speaker cabinet licensed from the Leslie Company and designed along the lines of Leslie's own Model 16. It carried a single 10-inch speaker behind a ported, rotating drum made from dense foam, with a footswitch for fast and slow speeds and on-off control. Guitarists had adapted traditional Leslie units for use in the past, but many felt that the rotating horn wasn't as flattering to the instrument's sound as the lower drum, with a traditional speaker. Also most Leslies had built-in amplifiers, which also weren't many guitarists' first choice for tone.

The Vibratone, on the other hand, was designed to be patched between a traditional guitar amplifier and speaker cabinet, with a crossover network that switched your signal back to the latter when the rotary unit was switched off. The Beatles and Pink Floyd both used

Vibratone cabinets prominently in the studio, and some years later Stevie Ray Vaughan slathered one all over his *Couldn't Stand the Weather* album, most prominently on the song "Cold Shot," as well as on the title track.

A year after introducing the Vibratone, Fender entered the effects pedal market properly—if you don't count the volume pedal it had offered in one form or another since the late 1940s—with the Fuzz-Wah and Fender Blender. Both were considered good-sounding pedals, and the latter went on to become a cult classic.

While the Fuzz-Wah's function was self-explanatory, the Blender was actually a combination of fuzz and octave pedals, uniquely merged and given a versatile set of four controls to govern them, plus a bonus second footswitch to kick in a hairy "Tone Boost" setting, resulting in a pedal that sounded like no other on the market at the time (or after, for that matter). George Harrison purportedly used a Fender Blender on his 1970 solo album *All Things Must Pass*, in particular on the song "What Is Life," but it is most prominently heard in Robin Trower's "Too Rolling Stoned" and other tracks from the 1974 album *Bridge of Sighs*.

The original Fender Blender was discontinued in 1977 but was later discovered by groundbreaking alt-rock guitarists such as Kevin Shields of My Bloody Valentine and Billy Corgan of the Smashing Pumpkins. Inspired, perhaps, by its cult noisemaker success, Fender reissued the four-knob Blender in 2005.

OPPOSITE: *A silverface Bassman head powers a Vibratone rotating-speaker cabinet.*
BELOW LEFT: *An original Fender Blender fuzz-octave pedal.*
BELOW RIGHT: *The Fender Fuzz Wah pedal.*

A Bevvy of Fancy Telecasters

Although long associated with the company's roots in the country-and-western scene, Fender chose the Telecaster as the platform for several variations on the form in the late 1960s. Unlike those that would follow, however, the first was clandestine—and entirely practical. In 1967, as the demand for popular tonewoods like ash and alder grew, Fender tried reducing the weight of several Telecasters by routing out much

of the body beneath the pickguard. The brief run of instruments, which otherwise had a standard-issue look with their pickguards on, became known as "Smuggler's Teles," given their convenient hidey-holes to, er, stash any contraband you might want to sneak past the authorities.

In 1968 Fender made a virtue of this routing by introducing the Telecaster

Thinline (later reversed as the Thinline Telecaster). Available in ash or mahogany, the Thinline's body was routed with three chambers from the back, which was then capped with a solid slice of wood. An f-hole was carved into the upper bout of the front. The Thinline was also given a fancy new pearloid pickguard, but otherwise it had the same pickup and control layout as the traditional Telecaster.

The single f-hole on the 1968 Thinline Telecaster's mahogany body declares the guitar's chambered status. Originally the headstock didn't carry the full model name.

Also in 1968, amid a turbulent political scene and ongoing protests against the Vietnam War—and some lingering hope that flower-power culture might present a way forward for young Americans— Fender introduced of the Paisley Red and Blue Flower Telecaster and Telecaster Bass. Both were standard examples of their respective models, equipped with complementary maple-cap necks and decorated with pinkish-red paisley or blue floral "finishes."

The effect was, in fact, created by the application of a product called Cling-Foil, made by Borden Chemical in Columbus, Ohio. This material had brightly colored patterns printed on the front of adhesive-backed foil that could be applied to walls, cabinets, home crafts, or, in this case, guitars. The guitars' body edges were finished to match the color of the appliqué and the entire thing was sprayed in a clear coat to protect the effort (the yellowing of which over time usually makes the underlying silver foil appear gold on vintage examples). A Plexiglas pickguard avoided hiding any of the guitars' paisley glory.

Hippies of the day never quite trucked into Fender dealers in droves to buy these bright, bold Teles, and the decorative process proved tricky and laborious—the clear coat often failed to adhere suitably to the Cling-Foil—and the model was dropped after 1969. One did end up in Tele supremo James Burton's hands for a time during his stint with Emmylou Harris, and country virtuoso Brad Paisley was virtually required by law to play one upon his arrival on the scene many years later.

"I started listening to Buck Owens with Don Rich, Roy Nichols with Merle Haggard, and James Burton with Elvis Presley and Ricky Nelson, and all those guys played Telecasters. So I just *wanted* a Tele, you know?"

BILL KIRCHEN Interview with Dave Hunter, December 2011

OPPOSITE LEFT: *A 1968 Paisley Red Telecaster.* OPPOSITE TOP: *A 1968 Paisley Red Telecaster Bass rests on a new-old-stock roll of the original Cling-Foil by Borden Chemical.* OPPOSITE BOTTOM: *A close look at the pattern on the Cling-Foil applied to a 1968 Paisley Red Telecaster Bass.* ABOVE RIGHT: *James Burton plays his 1990 signature model Telecaster while his original 1968 Paisley Tele looks on.* RIGHT: *Country star Brad Paisley and the only Telecaster he is legally certified to play.*

In 1967 Fender had also slipped a new student model into the lineup. The Bronco shared the Mustang's body shape and 24-inch scale length, with a single pickup in the bridge position and yet another new vibrato design, making six vibrato units on the seven guitars that carried them (Coronado included). The accompanying Bronco amplifier was essentially a 6-watt 1×8 Vibro Champ under a different name, with an advanced makeover of the new silver control panel that would soon grace the entire lineup.

LEFT: A red Bronco guitar leans on a Bronco amp in a youth-themed Fender ad shoot. OPPOSITE TOP: A special edition based on the Rosewood Telecaster Roger Rossmeisl created for George Harrison in 1968. OPPOSITE BOTTOM: A 1968 silverface Bassman head with "drip edge" grille, much like the one delivered to the Beatles rooftop concert.

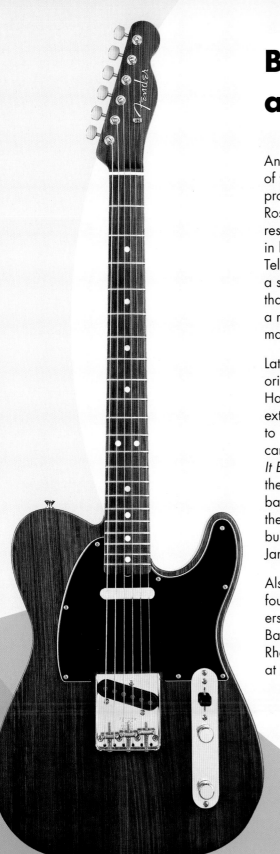

Booty for the Beatles and Silverface Amps

Another rare and short-lived Telecaster of the post-CBS era arrived as two prototypes made in 1968 by Roger Rossmeisl and Phillip Kubicki, later a respected custom guitar and bass maker in his own right. Named the Rosewood Telecaster for obvious reasons, each was a standard variation of the model, other than having a solid rosewood neck and a rosewood sandwich body with a thin maple center section.

Later that year Fender gifted one of the original Rosewood Telecasters to George Harrison, and the model went into extremely limited production from 1969 to 1972. Harrison's Rosewood Telecaster can be heard on much of the Beatles *Let It Be* album, but even before that release the guitar was used prominently in the band's famous final live performance, the rooftop concert atop the Apple building at 3 Saville Row in London on January 30, 1969.

Also present at this historic outing were four of Fender's new silverface amplifiers—three Twin Reverb combos and a Bassman stack—along with a Fender Rhodes Suitcase piano and amp, played at the show by session pianist Billy

Preston. Fender amplifiers had taken on a shiny new silver control panel in 1968, along with—for one year only—a strip of aluminum trim around the speaker baffle and grille cloth that became known as a drip edge.

The circuits inside these amps didn't change much initially, but as good as the silverface amplifiers would remain, they also signaled a decline in collectability following the blackface era. In years to come, CBS changed the electronic designs further in the name of efficiency, headroom, and—so it was claimed—reliability, but players would by and large come to prefer the sound of the earlier blackface amps. Many would convert their late-1960s and 1970s models to match those specifications.

As had so often been the case in Fender's history thus far, many product changes snuck in rather gradually, while others happened virtually overnight. As this "progress" plowed on through the 1970s, however, it became clear that much of this change was for the worse. The company faced a difficult reckoning coming out the other side of the new decade.

Chapter

10

SAVED BY THE BILL

Declining Quality and a Management Buyout

Riding high through the last few years of the 1960s, Fender was arguably the world's most successful and best recognized musical instrument manufacturer. What's more, the company's flagship electric guitar had been the main squeeze of the most dynamic and inventive guitarist yet to hit the rock scene, Jimi Hendrix. Hendrix's use of a Stratocaster as his primary instrument not only showed the world how versatile and expressive this design could be in the right hands: it also delivered a massive free dose of publicity.

When Hendrix squeezed out his ground-breaking live performance of "The Star-Spangled Banner" on an Olympic White Stratocaster at Woodstock in August 1969, it might have seemed to the guitar world at large that everything was going right for Fender. Despite this watershed moment, big changes were underway at the CBS-owned company. The early to mid-1970s at Fender would go on to offer some high points, but those who could read the tea leaves saw the lows coming. They hit hard later in the decade; come the next, they would threaten the company's very existence.

MAIN:
A 1973 Stratocaster in natural finish embodied several changes of the period.

RIGHT:
A fanciful piece typical of Fender advertising collateral in the 1970s.

THE COLLECTED WORKS OF FENDER

The End of Another Era: Don Randall's Departure

Although he declared that product quality hadn't declined in the first few years of CBS's ownership, Don Randall seems to have become progressively dissatisfied with the massive corporation's running of his company. He ultimately departed in 1969, several months before the official end of his five-year contract.

"CBS did so many things," Randall said many years later, "if I may say so, stupid things. They took some of our equipment that we'd paid a whole lot of money for, and because they didn't really know how to operate it, they put it out in the back lot and let it rust and go to pot. Thousands and thousands of dollars of specialized equipment."[46]

In a 2006 interview for the NAMM Oral Histories project, Randall further recalled:

Everything seemed to start falling apart. . . . When they were dickering with me to buy the company, they were gung-ho about everything, and they were the first two years that I ran the company for them. It came out pretty well. Then they got all these idiots that they had working for them in New York started finding excuses to come out to the West Coast, you know, big trip. It just screwed up the whole detail.

We ran a very tight ship, very tight. Leo was a very conservative type guy, and after he got out of

there they came out and we must have had three or four times the number of guys in the engineering department that we had before, because they were doing things that were just plain stupid, absolutely stupid. And I couldn't talk them out of it because they were, "Oh, well we're a big company and we should be able to do this, blah blah."

It finally made me sick to my stomach. I don't know that I regretted it, but I sure hated what had gone on with it. I almost doubled the sales the second year of the CBS deal, and then it just started going to hell, because I don't think that I had the feeling for it that I had before and all, because these guys were a bunch of idiots. Nice enough guys as individuals, but when it came to something like this, here they're coming out of the broadcasting business and sticking their nose in the music business. They didn't know a thing about it. It was just disgusting.[47]

Although he'd been "just the sales guy," as we've seen time and again, Don Randall had played a significant part in product development over his three decades with Fender, and he also deserved a lot of credit for helping these once-radical new instruments fly in the marketplace. As Fender prepared to enter what would be a tumultuous new decade, it did so without him.

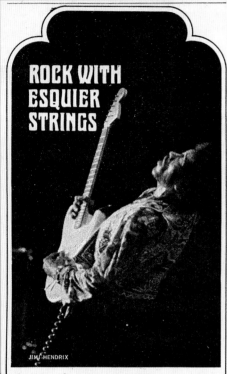

ROCK WITH ESQUIER STRINGS

JIMI HENDRIX

The string with the snappy magnetic response. Made of the finest alloys for prolonged playing life—precision wound for maximum resistance to stretch and pull. Available at your nearest music dealer.

For a Free String Catalog write to V. C. Squier, 427 Capital Avenue S.W., Battle Creek, Mich. 49016

Esquier Strings

V. C. SQUIER

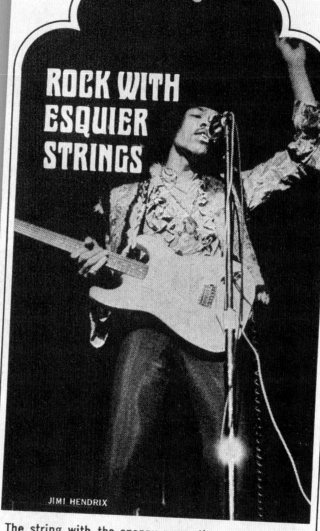

ROCK WITH ESQUIER STRINGS

JIMI HENDRIX

The string with the snappy magnetic response. Made of the finest alloys for prolonged playing life—precision wound for maximum resistance to stretch and pull. Available at your nearest music dealer. For Free String Catalog write V.C. Squier, Dept. BL-11, 427 Capital Ave. S.W., Battle Creek, Mich. 49016

V.C. **Squier**

Since 1890

*Jimi Hendrix revels in Squier strings'
"snappy magnetic response" in these
1969 ads.*

Pot-Metal Bridges and Three-Bolt Necks

This 1973 Stratocaster in natural finish displays several changes introduced in the early 1970s, including the redesigned bridge saddles, "bullet" headstock, and three-bolt neck attachment.

On the heels of the PR-coup-from-heaven represented by Jimi Hendrix's use of the Stratocaster before his death in 1970, following Eric Clapton's own uptake of the Strat as his main squeeze thereafter, and about a year and a half into Fender's run absent the guidance of Don Randall, the company decided to change several significant aspects of its flagship guitar's construction and components, largely to the detriment of overall quality in the eyes (and ears and hands) of many guitarists.

The first slew of changes hit in the fall of 1971. These included a new three-screw neck attachment with Tilt Neck adjustment facility, along with a headstock-end truss-rod adjustment nut shaped like a chromed bullet (hence the nickname "bullet headstock" that later stuck with these '70s Strats). In theory these might have been considered innovations: the Tilt Neck eliminated the need to shim a neck in the pocket to achieve a steeper angle, and thus a proper setup, and the bullet headstock abolished the need to remove the neck in order to make truss-rod adjustments. Actually, though, they became symbolic of Stratocasters plagued by declining quality in other regards.

Nearer the end of that year, Fender dispensed with the vibrato bridge's cold-rolled-steel inertia block and bent-steel saddles—originally designed by Leo and Freddie Tavares—and replaced both with components made from diecast Mazak (a.k.a. Zamak). This pot-metal alloy of zinc, aluminum, magnesium, and copper made for cheaper and easier component fabrication, but many guitarists found it detrimental to the Stratocaster's sustain and lively, ringing overall tone, in a change to what is often described as a thinner, lighter, and brighter voice.

Whatever your perspective, the Fender Stratocaster from the pre-CBS years up into the late 1960s was an undeniable classic. By the end of 1971, though, a Strat just didn't sound quite the same as one that had rolled off the line at the start of the year. Even so, countless Stratocasters from the 1970s have been used to make great music, and Ritchie Blackmore, Robin Trower, and the Edge all logged major hits on these otherwise less-collectible models.

The Wide Range Humbucker

Fender had hired former Gibson engineer Seth Lover in 1967. With the humbucking pickup proving more popular in heavy rock, it made perfect sense to task the cocreator of the legendary PAF humbucker with designing a unit suitable for the company's guitars. More than simply revamping the Gibson formula, though, Lover went to work on a unit that would preserve Fender's clear, articulate tone while also thickening the sound, adding drive, and, of course, rejecting the hum.

The Wide Range Humbucking Pickup was ready by 1970 and appeared on the Telecaster Thinline of 1971. The following year, the Telecaster Custom was reconfigured with one humbucker at the neck position and a new four-control layout and toggle-style pickup selector switch, while losing the body binding that had defined the model since 1959.

Many blues, rock, and jazz players had been modifying Teles for years by adding a humbucker in the neck position for a thicker, warmer tone, and the update of the Custom was clearly a bid to appeal to that market. The Telecaster Deluxe was also introduced in 1972, with the same switching array used on the revamped Custom, humbucking pickups in *both* neck and bridge positions, an enlarged Stratocaster-style headstock, and optional Strat-style vibrato.

Although these were very different Telecasters, many also became 1970s-era classics. The humbuckers and revised control layouts addressed the needs of heavier rockers and blues players of the era, but Telecaster Customs and Thinlines became even bigger successes via the used market in the punk and later grunge eras, when they often proved relatively affordable secondhand Fenders capable of making a big noise.

Notable guitarists who have done just that include Dave Pirner of Soul Asylum, a longtime devotee of the Telecaster Custom, along with Peter Buck in the early years of R.E.M. Keith Richards started subbing one in for the similarly appointed "Micawber"—a 1954 Telecaster with added neck humbucker—when the '72 Custom became available.

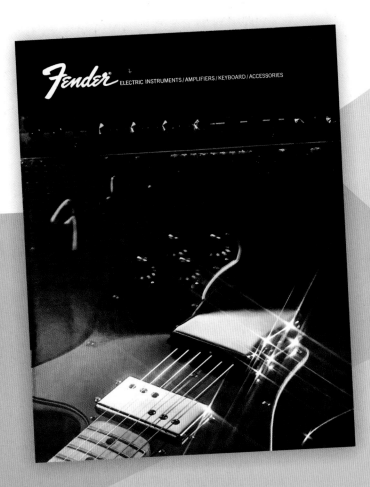

RIGHT: *The cover of the 1970 catalog displays a new Telecaster Custom with Wide Range humbucker, a component that would help define Fender innovations in the early '70s.* OPPOSITE LEFT: *The 1972 Telecaster Thinline gets a makeover with dual Wide Range humbuckers and six-saddle bridge.* OPPOSITE RIGHT: *A 1977 Telecaster Custom with ash body in natural finish.*

Raging Success and Some Shakeups

Sales and production continued to increase dramatically throughout the 1970s. In 1976 Fender had expanded into an enormous 5-acre facility in Fullerton where more than 750 employees churned out a wide range of products. By 1979 Fender was selling forty thousand guitars a year, and in 1980 the company had tripled the $20 million-a-year income that Don Randall had boasted about from the previous decade.

Despite this clear success, something was clearly and drastically wrong with the formula. CBS was reinvesting little of the profits into maintaining production standards, and for all the profits, the company actually began losing money by the early 1980s. Around this time, Fender dropped the Mustang, Bronco, and Telecaster Deluxe and Custom from the lineup; they also ditched the short-lived second shot at a semihollow electric, the Starcaster, which had run from 1976 to 1979.

Meanwhile the company tried several variations on the Stratocaster format for the first time, testing the waters with the 25th Anniversary Stratocaster in 1979, the Strat in 1980, and the limited Gold/Gold Stratocaster in 1981—the latter two returning to the slimmer Stratocaster headstock, albeit one not cut to a shape representative of the original from the 1950s, thanks to worn-out or misplaced tooling.

Also in 1981 Fender introduced the Bullet series, a new student line designed by John Page. Page had started at Fender in 1978 and advanced from the shop floor to the design team, working

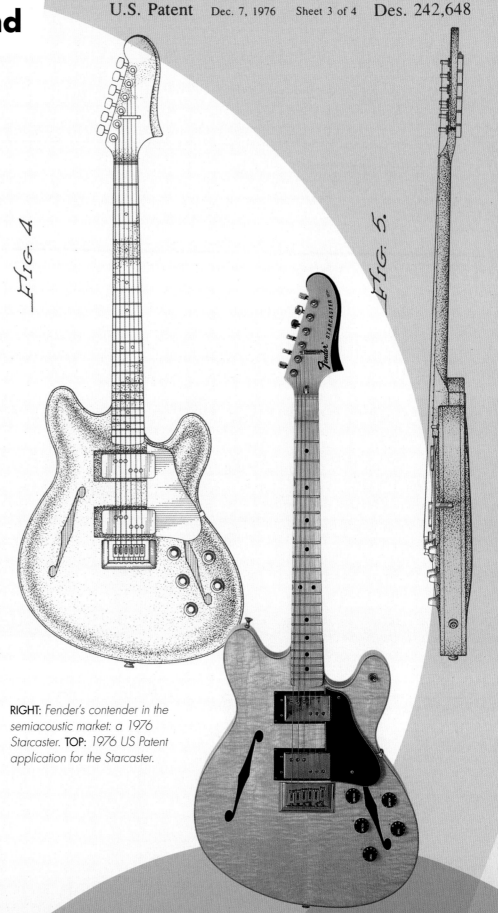

Fig. 4.

Fig. 5.

RIGHT: *Fender's contender in the semiacoustic market: a 1976 Starcaster.* TOP: *1976 US Patent application for the Starcaster.*

LEFT: *A 1979 25th Anniversary Stratocaster.*
CENTER: *A 1980 Strat model: modernized features, but a return to the small headstock—sort of.*
RIGHT: *The 1981 Bullet, a minimalist Tele-inspired student guitar designed by John Page.*

alongside the legendary Freddie Tavares, among others. Following some quality hiccups after having some of the Bullets' initial components manufactured in Korea to save money, all-US manufacture restored impressive quality to these affordable, Tele-inspired single-cut models, and they have remained popular on the used market over the years.

"I remember my directive from marketing was to design a guitar that could be manufactured for $65 in manufacturing cost," Page said, "and I think I came within a dollar of that, and it retailed for $199 at the time. . . . It was a really cool first product for me to design, and it's funny that it's hip again!"[48]

Reviving the Lineup

The Stratocaster headstock revision represented a shift in thinking at Fender, which arrived courtesy of a big shakeup in the company's management. In an effort to restore the company's reputation in 1981, CBS hired three young executives from the US branch of Japanese instrument manufacturer Yamaha: Bill Schultz was made president of Fender, John McLaren was named head of the CBS Musical Instruments Division, and Dan Smith was hired as director of marketing for electric guitars. After assessing the situation on the ground, the new management team set about revising the product line—starting with the Stratocaster—but they found they had some obstacles to overcome to get there.

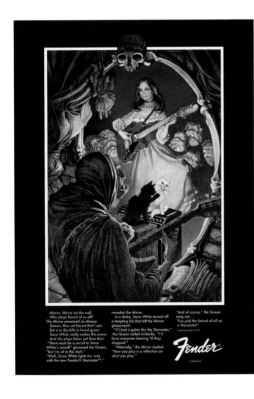

> "When I first saw a Stratocaster properly I realized that it's a thing of sculpted beauty. If you look at the cross section, I mean, that could be something flying through space, to me. It's a utilitarian thing, but it's beautiful."

MARK KNOPFLER BBC Interview, November 2008

Fender's often fairy tale–themed promotional efforts from the 1970s.

"I am precisely three inches high," said the Caterpillar, "though I frequently become much higher."

"With that magic mushroom?" Alice asked eagerly.

"With music!" retorted the Caterpillar, conjuring visions of Fender® guitars and matching amplifiers. "I play inhumanly hot licks on my Stratocaster® and back myself with everything else."

"But I have only two arms," sighed Alice, "If I am to reach new heights on a Strat®, I shall need your backing on electric bass."

"On a *Fender!*" smiled the Caterpillar. "Or two or three. I should much rather get my hands on what TV concert bassmen play."

"And of course," Alice sang out ... "9 out of 10 pick a Fender bass!"

Originally printed in 1975

© 2006 FMIC

The world's favorite love machine

Love makes the world go round. Music sets the mood, heightens the emotion and provides the beat. Love takes two. Fender® guitars and amps are compatible—made for each other. If you really want to make it, in love or music, try a little Fenderness.

For a full-color 64-page Fender Catalog, plus a full-color 22" X 25" poster version of this ad, send $1.00 for postage and handling to Fender, Box 3410, Dept. O-4, Fullerton, California 92634.

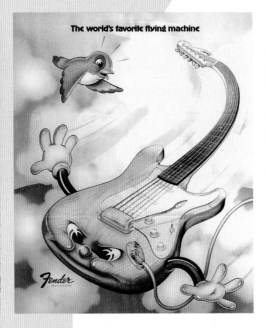

The world's favorite flying machine

The world's favorite recording machine

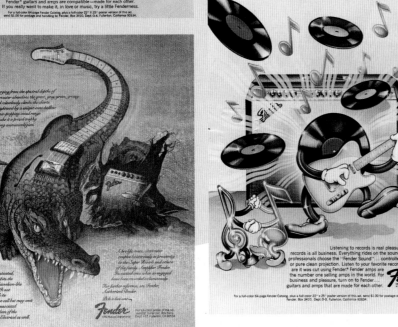

First heard emerging from the spectral depths of creation in 1976, Starcaster abandons the green, gray-green, & may Lazophye and relentlessly climbs the charts. Its attack is heightened by a unique non-deflective body and jaw-popping sustain range which make it a prized trophy among animal enthusiasts.

When domesticated, Starcaster exhibits the most deceptive, chameleon-like vocal qualities. It not only believes forth its own unique call but may emit musical tones associated with other members of the species Guitar Electrical as well.

A terrific-sized Starcaster couples heartwarmingly in proximity to the Super Reverb and others of the family—Amplifier Fender. The contact even when so engaged have been recorded extemporarily.

For further reference, see Fender Authorized Dealer.

Pick a live one.

The Hard-Charging Sharp-Toothed Starcaster
(Xstrogator Fender)

Listening to records is real pleasure. Making records is all business. Everything rides on the sound, and more professionals choose the "Fender Sound"... controlled distortion or pure clean projection. Listen to your favorite record. Chances are it was cut using Fender® amps are the number one selling amps in the world. For business and pleasure, turn on to Fender... guitars and amps that are made for each other.

For a full-color 64-page Fender Catalog, plus a full-color 22" x 25" poster version of this ad, send $1.00 for postage and handling to Fender, Box 3410, Dept. O-3, Fullerton, California 92634.

*Intended as "modern" at the time, Fender's 1970s ads generally haven't weathered as well as those from the 1950s and 1960s. **OPPOSITE:** The 1982 catalog documents Fender's transition through several eras of classics.*

"We took it for granted that they could make Stratocasters and Telecasters the way they used to make them," Smith recalled. "But we were wrong. So many things had been changed in the plant."[49]

Similarly Schultz later recalled, "CBS allowed the company to deteriorate—the products, the quality. But when I took over, they gave me millions of dollars to put back into R&D, to put into equipment, and we brought the quality level back up."[50]

Players continued to recognize the quality, superb playing feel, and high sonic integrity of earlier Fender guitars and amplifiers, those from the pre-CBS period in particular. By the early 1980s, British guitarist Mark Knopfler had brought the wiry, exciting sound of his Fiesta Red 1961 Stratocaster to the forefront of popular music via several hits with his band Dire Straits; Stevie Ray Vaughan was just starting to set the blues world alight on a battered '62 Strat; and Bruce Springsteen had tramped his blond '50s Telecaster through arenas around the world after memorializing it on the cover of his 1975 album *Born to Run* and using it as his main squeeze thereafter. Vintage specs were where it was at, and the new team devised a plan to get Fender back there.

The plan: Fender personnel would study the creations of their counterparts of more than twenty years prior in an effort to reinvent the wheel.

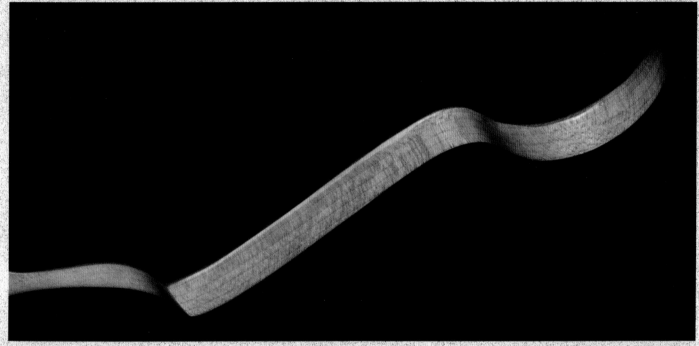

THE SOUND THAT CREATES LEGENDS

"Dan Smith and I traveled to a big vintage guitar store in Illinois," recalled John Page, "to check out as many vintage Fenders guitars as we could. We recorded lots of specs, took tons of photos, and bought several to bring back to the factory with us."[51]

Meanwhile Fender longtimer Freddie Tavares had already been working on a vintage-spec 1952 Telecaster reissue, which joined the team's '57 Stratocaster with maple fingerboard and '62 Stratocaster with rosewood fingerboard in the new Vintage Reissue series.

Production launched simultaneously in the US and at the Fujigen Gakki factory in Japan (the latter initially intended for the domestic Japanese market only), and the Japanese manufacturing got up to speed more quickly and hit the streets first. Smith, Schultz, and McClaren quickly took advantage of this unforeseen potential to speed production and distribution.

Big in Japan and a Sale in America

While Fender retooled for improved production in Fullerton in 1982, Fender Japan Co. Ltd., founded in the spring of that year, began a series of Vintage Reissue guitars that would initially sell in Asia and Europe. For a short time, these bore the full-sized Fender logo with the distinguishing "Squier Series" beneath it, adapting the name of the Squier string company, which Fender had acquired in the late 1960s. That was soon changed to a larger Squier logo, and then "Squier by Fender" a short while after. Although the venture was initially intended to provide some breathing room as the new management of the American Fender operation settled in, the Squier range introduced an enduring line of more affordable guitars, while the early examples—long recognized for their quality—have become collectible in their own right.

ROCK WITH ESQUIER STRINGS

The string with the snappy magnetic response. Made of the finest alloys for prolonged playing life—precision wound for maximum resistance to stretch and pull. Available at your nearest music dealer. For Free String Catalog write V. C. Squier, Dept. IM, 427 Capital Ave. S.W., Battle Creek, Mich. 49015.

Esquier Strings

International Musician/Feb. 1969/5025

CONCERT MASTER STRINGS BY SQUIER

Designed for artists who insist on responsive resonance and perfectly balanced tone quality. Individually wound, inspected and selected. Concert Master Strings are crafted from the finest materials—imported steel, hand polished and perfectly tinned gut, wound with spun aluminum, or pure silver. Once used by the artist, no other string will satisfy his musical ear. Concert Master, the most respected name in bowed strings, includes Violin, Viola, Violoncello and Double Bass Strings. For Free Catalog Write Dept. 15-S, 427 Capital Ave., V.C. S.W. Battle Creek. Mich 49016.

SQUIER Since 1890

THE INSTRUMENTALIST
June 1968
Job #4646

LEFT: *A 1983 Japanese Squier by Fender '62 Stratocaster in Fiesta Red.* **ABOVE:** *Fender's acquisition of the V. C. Squier string company (sometimes branded Esquier) in the 1960s would provide a brand name for a new, more affordable series of guitars.*

ABOVE: *Headstocks from a run of Squier guitars as the brand transitioned from "Fender Squier Series" to "Squier by Fender."* BELOW: *The Squier name took second billing on Fender's first made-in-Japan electric guitars.*

Despite the introduction of the popular and much-improved Vintage Reissue series the following year—and a wholesale effort to revive the quality of Fender guitars and other products (not entirely derailed by a handful of coinciding misfires in the downgraded Strat and Tele models and the arguably misguided Elite series)—CBS had apparently grown weary of the guitar business by 1984. Much as Leo Fender and Don Randall had done twenty years before, the broadcasting giant began looking for a buyer.

The trouble was potential buyers were acting cagey and offering short money for the big name in electric guitars. The guitar industry was in flux worldwide: punk, new wave, and hair metal had changed the guitar landscape, while the synthesizer threatened to replace electric string instruments entirely. Plus Asian guitar production had become more accepted in Western markets.

None of the big companies courting Fender seemed prepared to make offers that would be more profitable than simply going into liquidation, so CBS proposed that the executive team raise the funds to purchase the company themselves. On March 5, 1985, CBS sold Fender for $12.5 million to a management group headed by Bill Schultz, who became CEO of the newly formed Fender Musical Instrument Co. (FMIC).

Some years later, Schultz recalled his rationale for taking the leap and purchasing the floundering company: "Fender has a great name, a great founder. All we had to do was follow his philosophy. We work under the premise that you've got to look ahead and make changes—you have to keep innovating, creating, and developing—but you can never forget your past. And our past was Leo Fender. It was a lot of fun to follow somebody like that."[52]

The management group, which included Dan Smith and other significant Fender execs, had a deep trough to climb out of. The purchase price was $500,000 less than CBS had paid for Fender twenty years earlier (before adjustment for inflation): that might seem like a bargain for the massive company, but it excluded most of the Fender machinery and many patents, as well as the Fullerton factory, which was sold separately. The new, trimmed-down Fender was instantly roughly $11 million in debt and would have to subsist mainly on Japanese manufacturing while getting FMIC's new facilities up and running.

But the historic Fender name had been saved. With creative and insightful management, the future looked brighter for the legendary brand than it had for some time.

OPPOSITE: *Fender players and execs. Back row (from left): Hal Lindes, Dan Smith, Bill Schultz, Jeff Beck, and David Gilmour. Front row (from left): Stuart Adamson, Eric Clapton, Hank Marvin, Steve Howe, and Richard Thompson.* **ABOVE:** *Dan Smith (left) is largely credited with restoring Fender guitars to vintage-correct specifications in the 1980s.*

Chapter 11

HOT ROD ROCK

The Custom Shop and Relic Guitars

With the Fullerton factory excluded from its purchase of the Fender brand in 1985, FMIC set about building a new facility in Corona, California. Once that was underway, CEO Bill Schultz was eager to remind the guitar world how good a Fender could be.

Schultz decided to establish a "best-of-the-best" department, a hot rod shop where custom-grade luthiers would craft the finest renditions of both traditional Fender models and adventurous new designs to suit the needs of name artists and special-order clients alike. This department would be called the Fender Custom Shop, and Schultz tasked FMIC vice president Dan Smith with setting it up.

Guitar players the world over, and Fender fans in particular, are well aware of the high quality of instruments that the Fender Custom Shop has turned out since 1987. But consider how young the newly reconstructed Fender company was when this elite department was established, and it's clear the Custom Shop had to hit the ground running—no false starts allowed—to make the venture work. To do that, Smith needed a couple of top-notch luthiers to head up the operation, and he knew just where to find them.

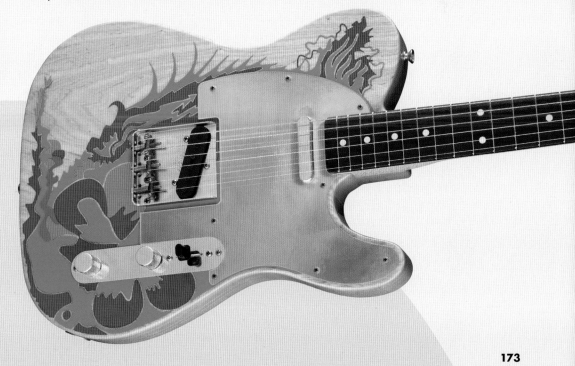

Paging Michael Stevens

The first candidate for one of these positions was Michael Stevens. Stevens had begun his career in the late 1960s working at the famed Guitar Resurrection in San Francisco, a first stop for major Bay Area guitarists in need of repair and custom work. Having returned some years later to his native Texas, he took a detour for several years to train Arabian show horses at a ranch in remote McKinney, Texas. Picking up luthiery again in 1978, Stevens opened his own workshop in Austin, where he repaired—and eventually built—guitars for Stevie Ray and Jimmie Vaughan, Otis Rush, Albert King, Eric Johnson, Lonnie Mack, Hubert Sumlin, Junior Brown, and other guitar legends.

"Fast-forward to the '80s," Stevens recalls, "and I'd built the famous double-neck for Christopher Cross, the Git-Steel for Junior Brown, my own Classic design, the Paul Glasse Model electric mandolin, and the Roscoe Beck six-string bass, most notably used on the bass solo on Robben Ford's 'Talk to Your Daughter.' I was at NAMM [in the mid-1980s], and Robben was very tight with Dan Smith from Fender, so Roscoe brought him by to meet me and see another bass I had there."[53]

Following the NAMM show, Smith got in touch with Stevens to discuss using him as a consultant at Fender, to ask about licensing his designs and to run through some early ideas for the Custom Shop concept. Having also just won best of show for a custom Flying V-style guitar in the Dallas Guitar Show of 1986, Stevens was also being courted by Gibson for its own burgeoning custom department.

Stevens weighed the offers and, as he succinctly puts it, "I took the Fender job."

Knowing that Stevens would need an assistant in the challenge, Smith suggested an insider with some knowledge of the company and recommended John Page, who had already helped him with returning Fender's core models closer to vintage spec shortly before the change of ownership. The only trick was, Page wasn't actually a Fender employee at that point in 1986, and Stevens had never met him.

Hired by Fender under CBS in 1978, Page recalls, he

> had spent close to nine years in guitar R&D, three as a model maker and six as a guitar design engineer with Freddie Tavares. I had left Fender at the end of January of 1986 to spend the year in the studio working on my music, but I did some design consulting for Fender as well. By around November of that year, I realized that I was going to have to go back to work somewhere, so I contacted Dan Smith and asked him if there were any openings.

> Dan gave me the choice of going back into Guitar R&D, the position I had left in January, or working with Michael Stevens in the Custom Shop. Although we had discussed opening the Custom Shop many years prior, Bill had finally decided to make it happen. I thought that would be pretty cool, so I chose the latter.[54]

As the first man in, Stevens could nix the choice if he didn't feel that Page fit, but, as he recalls: "Page and I hit it off quickly, and I realized I needed his knowledge of Fender. Done!"

Fender wanted to show off some Custom Shop product in the upcoming 1987 Winter NAMM show, just two months away; without an official shop to work in, the team got right down to it, working out of the cluttered R&D Model Shop in Brea, California. After completing a pair of Stratocasters for Eric Johnson and another for Eric Clapton, Custom Shop builds for Pete Townshend and David Gilmour were next in line. Soon Yngwie Malmsteen, Elliot Easton, Caesar Rosas, Danny Gatton, Robert Cray, Waylon Jennings, and a host of others were also Custom Shop clients. Shortly after, the Custom Shop also generated Fender's first American-made set-neck guitar, the Stevens-designed LJ (only thirty were built in the US, but several more were later made by Fender Japan).

RIGHT: *John Page, left, and Michael Stevens.* BELOW: *Neck templates line a section of wall in the Custom Shop.*

The Best of the Best

Fender management had first viewed the Custom Shop as a small showcase—a jewel in the crown of the FMIC operation as a whole—but that attitude quickly changed once the department's potential became clear.

"I don't think [Schultz] ever saw it growing to the extent that we ultimately did," said Page. "He wanted us to be able to build anything that people wanted, and I think he saw us as being able to lift the overall quality image of Fender."[55]

Stevens concurs: "Bill Schultz told me, 'If we can only break even, I want the coolest Custom Shop on the planet!' We did that and put Fender back on the map."[56]

About six months into the operation, it was clear that the Custom Shop was going to do better than break even: it would thrive, making a considerable profit for FMIC.

"I guess around 1989," says Page, "it finally occurred to me that we were indeed writing a new chapter in Fender's history. That's also about the same time that my mentor, Freddie Tavares, came by to visit and told me that the shop reminded him of when he first started working for Leo Fender in the 1950s. That was monumental to me!"[57]

A decade after its inception, the Custom Shop had grown into its own 30,000-square-foot premises filled with sixty employees, a roster that included notable master builders like Chris Fleming, Fred Stuart, J. W. Black, John English, John Suhr, Stephen Stern, Gene Baker, Mark Kendrick, George Blanda, and Alan Hamel, among others. Michael Stevens returned to Texas and an independent one-man shop of his own in 1990, and John Page left in 1998 to become executive director of the Fender

Museum of Music and the Arts Foundation. Mike Eldred took the helm upon Page's departure, beginning a long and successful tenure that lasted until his own departure in 2015, when Mike Lewis stepped into the job.

Having begun as Fender's best of the best, the Custom Shop has continued to live up to that reputation, while fulfilling the needs of a far larger number of customers than Stevens and Page likely could have imagined back in 1987. In doing so, it has truly lived up to both concepts of what a Custom Shop can be: a department crafting special-order guitars with custom or nonstandard features, and—as perhaps more Fender players have viewed it these past thirty-some years—the elite branch responsible for recapturing the best and most authentic of Fender's guitars of the 1950s and 1960s.

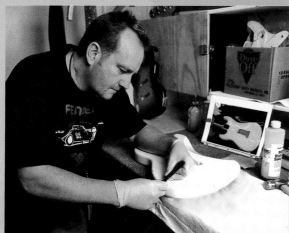

OPPOSITE: *Dan Smith in 2004.* **ABOVE LEFT:** *J. W. Black in the Custom Shop's wood stores in the early '90s.* **ABOVE RIGHT:** *Master builder Fred Stuart and a western-themed CS Telecaster.* **LEFT:** *Mike Eldred took the helm at the Custom Shop upon John Page's departure in 1998. He stayed on until 2015.*

Into the Time Machine

With Fender's American Vintage Reissue (AVRI) guitars gaining more respect in the marketplace alongside an enthusiastic uptake of the more contemporary American Standard models—which added modern features and upgrades to the traditional body and neck shapes—the creations of the Custom Shop were becoming recognized as the true elite of vintage-reproduction electric guitars. And with no sign of the craze for pre-CBS Fenders abating, the powers that be saw sense in making these great guitars look even more like the well-loved Stratocasters and Telecasters from the 1950s and 1960s craved by so many players.

The process of artificially aging, antiquing, or distressing an instrument has existed for decades. But the relic wasn't a thing until the Fender Custom Shop made it one. Prior to the introduction of the Relic Series in 1995, fake aging and wear was applied to guitars either to help repairs made to valuable old instruments match the look of the original or to create forgeries. You could say that Fender's famed Relics came about as a merger of these two—except that the shady latter undertaking was negated by the legitimate presence of the Fender name on the headstocks, along with a consistent effort to mark such guitars indelibly as Reissues.

The seeds for the Custom Shop's Relic Series were first sown in the early 1990s by J. Black, who had been hired by John Page to work in the Custom Shop in 1989. Black had learned to repair and restore guitars to a high level in a handful of previous positions, including a stint at the notable Roger Sadowsky Guitars shop in New York City.

"I saw Don Was at his studio on Mulholland Drive in LA when he was recording the Stones in the early '90s," says Black, "and he said he was attending the Grammys. Bonnie Raitt was nominated and he was her producer, and they were going to perform. He had a new bass and wanted to know if we could 'beat up' or distress the instrument so it wouldn't look like new sneakers on the playground."[58] (For the record, the oft-told story that Fender Relics began after Keith Richards said he'd play a new Custom Shop guitar if they'd "bashed it up a bit" is apocryphal, and has been thoroughly debunked by all parties involved.)

Afterward the Custom Shop occasionally applied a little aging treatment as one-offs for artists who needed that look, but it wouldn't be a standard line until the arrival of Vince Cunetto, an outsider who had become known for his uncanny ability to create authentically aged reproduction pre-CBS-style guitars.

MAIN: *A Custom Shop Relic Esquire.*
INSET: *Texas guitar hero Eric Johnson promotes the American Standard Stratocaster in this 1987 ad.*

The Cunetto Relics

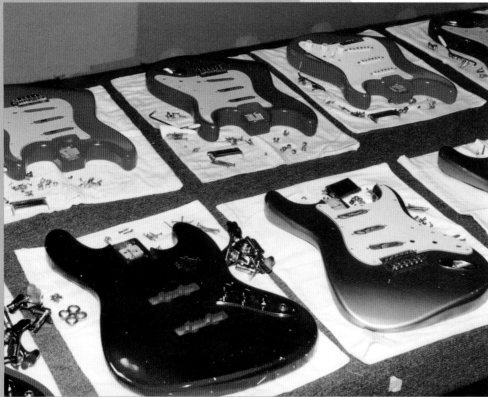

Vince Cunetto was a vintage-Fender enthusiast living and working in Kansas City, Missouri, when he was introduced to J. Black, who had also worked in Kansas City for a time before moving to the Custom Shop. By this time Cunetto had begun hand-aging parts and components to be used on reproduction-style guitars, and Black was impressed with what he saw. The pair stayed in touch, and through the early 1990s Black noted that Cunetto's reproduction guitars were getting good—alarmingly good. And that they'd also begun carrying the Fender name on the headstock, after Cunetto taught himself how to reproduce the vintage-style spaghetti logo decals.

Black called out Cunetto on the pirated logos and informed him there was only one way he could keep it up: if he officially built the guitars for the Fender Custom Shop. He requested a couple of samples, and the results were breathtaking.

"Vince sent John [Page] and I an aged '60s-style Strat in gold metallic," Black recalled. "All the parts and finish on the guitar were aged and patina'd to look like an authentic vintage instrument. It was very convincing and was on the cusp of being a counterfeit. We decided to use Vince to make a couple of proto-types for the [winter 1995] NAMM show: a '50s Nocaster in aged butter-scotch-blond, and an aged '57 Stratocaster in two-tone Sunburst."[59]

TOP: *Vince Cunetto matching up Relic bodies and hardware circa 1996.* BOTTOM: *Relic bodies and hardware in Cunetto's workshop.* OPPOSITE: *A pair of Vince Cunetto's early Fender Relic prototypes circa 1995.*

According to Cunetto,

By the time we did the NAMM samples, we didn't know how many we were going to sell or anything, but we just wanted a good sample of each one to show. We got those done, and John didn't tell anybody about it in management and all. He had two glass display cases made with gold plaques, and all it said on it was "'50s Relic Nocaster" and "'50s Relic Stratocaster." And I showed up at the NAMM show, because J. said, "You're gonna want to be here for this!" We hung them up, and people were saying, "Wow, that's really cool that you're paying an homage to your history with these old guitars!" And the reps were like, "Yeah, they're new guitars. How many do you want?" And that was it. That was it![60]

According to Page, Black, and Cunetto, Fender's head of marketing, Mike Lewis, was entirely supportive of the venture. "He embraced it right away," Cunetto adds. "He looked at [the Relics], and he was like, 'Hell yeah, we're going to do this! Who wouldn't want to play this? You could take this guitar at any time on any stage and put it in somebody's hand, and they'd say, "Yeah, I'll play that!"

TOP: *A 2006 Eric Clapton Blackie Tribute Stratocaster, with memorabilia in replica Anvil flight case.* **ABOVE:** *Matching components to the original "Brownie" in the Custom Shop.* **OPPOSITE:** *Eric Clapton in 2013 with the Custom Shop's "Brownie" re-creation.*

For the first few years of their existence, the Fender Relics were produced in Springfield, Missouri, by Cunetto and a team of "aging artists" that he trained himself. They'd finish and distress bodies, necks, and components sent by the boxload from the Custom Shop, returning the parts there afterward for final assembly. The line expanded to include the occasional bass, some Jazzmasters, and other Fender models—all done in aged versions of virtually every official Custom Color under the sun—along with several notable artist guitars for the likes of Sting, Eric Clapton, members of the Rolling Stones, and others.

LEFT TOP: *Nile Rogers with the Custom Shop Hitmaker Stratocaster.* **LEFT:** *Ike Turner and his gold Custom Shop Stratocaster.* **ABOVE:** *Reggie Hamilton and his Custom Shop Signature Jazz Bass.*

ABOVE: *Long-time Fender player Jeff Beck is the subject of a Custom Shop Signature Strat.*
RIGHT TOP: *Yngwie Malmsteen and Custom Shop Signature Stratocaster.* **RIGHT:** *Andy Summers and his Custom Shop Tribute Telecaster.*

The Hot Rod Shop Rolls On

In 1999 following John Page's departure the year before, production of the Relic Series was brought back in-house under Mike Eldred, the new head of the Custom Shop. Upon the operation's return, Eldred refreshed the lineup, introducing the popular Time Machine Series, which presented 1950s maple-board and 1960s rosewood-board Telecasters and Stratocasters, and Jazz and Precision Basses in three different levels of distress: Relic, Closet Classic (gently aged), and New Old Stock (or NOS, vintage-style, but unaged).

This three-tiered series had a long and successful run—although the Relics always sold in the greatest numbers—and has further evolved in recent years. Around the late 2000s and early 2010s, some custom orders and short runs were aged to what was termed Heavy Relic and Ultra Relic condition, adding increasing levels of distress to the existing gradations.

OPPOSITE: *A Custom Shop Jazzmaster.*
ABOVE: *Custom Shop Pete Townshend Strats on stage and ready to go.*

Upon Eldred's departure in 2015, Mike Lewis further expanded the Time Machine offerings to include (ranked in levels of aging from none to most): NOS, Closet Classic, Lush Closet Classic, Journeyman Relic, Relic, and Heavy Relic. Many players and product reviewers agree that the current range of Fender Relic models includes some of the finest predistressed guitars the Custom Shop has ever produced, while the guitars of the Cunetto Era remain highly prized and now carry collector-grade prices on the used market.

Formerly a successful and highly respected independent custom-guitar maker, Ron Thorn was hired by the Custom Shop in 2018 as a principal master builder and was named director of the Custom Shop a short time later.

"Fender might be a huge corporation, but it's still a hot-rod shop here," said Thorn. "These guys are still willing to take chances, and are digging it, and are cool about it. Everybody's a player—and let's put it this way: no one has said 'Don't do that' to me yet!"[61]

As acclaimed as the Custom Shop's work has been since its inception, Thorn's oversight and an ongoing push to make this "the best of the best" continues to elevate the quality and attention to detail seen in this department's output today. Long apparent in the elite Master Built guitars, such consistency and "next-level" achievement now plays through in all of the Custom Shop's team-built instruments as well. At the time of this writing, these are produced in six standard series: Vintage Custom, Artisan, Limited Edition, American Custom, Postmodern, and Time Machine, which are frequently joined by Limited Edition series and special runs for authorized Custom Shop dealers.

TOP: *Custom Shop master builder Ron Thorn.*
LEFT: *John Page at the Custom Shop in 1996.*
OPPOSITE: *A Custom Shop Troy Van Leeuwen Masterbuilt Doubleneck Jazzmaster.*

BORDER SONG

Fender Amps Roar Back

If the new owners' efforts to bring Fender guitars back to their former glory represented a major challenge, reviving amplifier production was an even more arduous task. The mass production of tube-based electronics, and the sourcing of heavy and expensive components involved in their manufacture, is a mammoth undertaking in the best of times. With no factory in which to seamlessly continue Fender's previous lines, FMIC was very much at sea for several years before a consistent new range could be brought to market.

Fortunately an impressive and well-regarded range of short-lived new Fender models had helped keep the brand name alive on amplifiers of the early 1980s, just as guitar production

was going through some of its rockiest times. From 1982 to 1985, Fender manufactured a series of tube amps designed by respected engineer Paul Rivera. These included the Champ II, Concert II, Deluxe Reverb II, Harvard Reverb II, Princeton Reverb II, Twin Reverb II, and Super Champ. All had hot-rodded preamps with higher gain than their original iterations, while many also had channel switching and pull-boost functions.

With CBS's sale of Fender to Schultz's team, however, the Rivera-designed amplifiers—which have, to some extent, become player's collectibles today—fell by the wayside, as the new owners struggled to keep an amp in the game through the transition years.

Red Knobs and Amplifier Reissues

As far as amplifier production is concerned, the newly independent FMIC survived the startup years of 1985 and 1986 mostly on the dregs of the CBS years and a few solid-state imports from Japan. Later in 1986 and early 1987 the first new American-made tube amps went into production in the form of the Champ 12, the Twin, and the Dual Showman. Manufacture of these red-knob amps—so called for the red knobs on their control panels—was made possible by FMIC's acquisition of the Sunn amplifier company (a line soon to be reissued in its own right) and its factory in Lake Oswego, Oregon, where many of the transition-era Fender amps would be produced.

In 1990, however, Fender saw the sense in giving its amp line the same treatment that had helped to revive the guitars in the 1980s: it was time for a reissue, and one of the all-time classics would lead the way.

Guitarists had long recognized the glories of Fender's tweed amps from the 1950s, with the 4×10 5F6-A Bassman combo of 1958–1960 being a particular favorite among many tone-conscious pro players. Fender took notice, and in 1990 the first of a popular and enduring line of reissue amplifiers was released: the '59 Bassman Vintage Reissue. This tweed classic was initially joined by the '63 Vibroverb Vintage Reissue, another combo that was a reincarnation of the 2×10 combo in light-brown Tolex that represented Fender's very first reverb-equipped amplifier. In 1992 Fender added to the Reissue series by bringing back another long-awaited classic in the guise of the '65 Twin Reverb Vintage Reissue, which similarly went a long way toward recapturing the sound and playing feel of a blackface Twin Reverb of the mid-1960s.

And it is worth noting, perhaps, since the chronology takes us there, that these Reissues were arriving just a year on either side of the passing of the amps' original creator; Leo Fender himself died on March 21, 1991, following a sustained career at the helm of other notable guitar and amplifier companies.

While continuing with the Reissues—a line that grew considerably in coming years—new amplifier production at Fender branched off in 1993 into two important new directions: the Custom Amp Shop and the Tweed Series.

OPPOSITE: *A small but mighty 1983 Super Champ designed by Paul Rivera.* ABOVE: *Installing the chassis in a tweed Bassman reissue.* LEFT: *Buddy Guy, Robert Cray, Jimmie Vaughan, and Eric Clapton play Strats through Reissue, vintage, and red-knob Fender amps.*

The former was what the name implies: a small-run shop (by Fender standards) that produced high-quality, hand-wired tube amps drawing inspiration from Fender classics of old, while adding new features essential to contemporary guitarists. One of the first two releases was the Vibro King, a 60-watt 3×10 combo in blond Tolex with brown control panel, featuring opto-cell tremolo and a built-in, slightly revised rendition of Fender's early-1960s three-knob Reverb Unit.

The other was the Tone Master, a whopping 100-watt head with foot-switchable Rhythm and Lead channels, paired with a big 4×12 speaker cabinet, both again in blond Tolex with brown control panels and oxblood grille cloth. Over the next few years, these were joined by the Prosonic and Dual Professional, which further proved that Fender tube amps were back to stay.

The new Tweed Series was rolled out from 1993 to 1995. This was essentially Fender's standard amp line, but it included a range of amps initially covered in 1950s-style diagonal tweed, another nod to Fender's glory years. Early offerings included the Pro Junior, Blues Junior, Blues Deluxe, and Blues De Ville, in ascending order of output power from 15 watts to 50 watts. In 1996 Fender added the Hot Rod Deluxe and Hot Rod Deville to the lineup. Now dressed in black Tolex—which others in the series later adopted, along with limited-edition colors and other cosmetics— these two had Lead channels modified for higher gain to suit their new monikers.

Over the years amps from this series have become enduring working guitarist's classics, appearing in venues large and small the world over, often hitting the road in the backlines of significant touring artists. As such they very ably stepped into the shoes of Fender amplifiers of the 1960s and 1970s—such as the Deluxe Reverb, Twin Reverb, and Super Reverb—to become the new standards of the late twentieth and early twenty-first centuries.

OPPOSITE: *The Vibro-King represents hand-wired Custom Shop quality.* TOP LEFT: *In 1996 Fender added the Hot Rod Deluxe and Hot Rod Deville, including limited-edition colors. This purple Deluxe is shown with the purple metalflake J Mascis Signature Jazzmaster.* TOP RIGHT: *Gary Clark Jr's trio of stacked 3×10 Vibro-King combos.*

South of the Border

ABOVE LEFT: *Stringing up a Stratocaster in the Ensenada factory.*
ABOVE RIGHT: *Mexican-made Fender necks ready to meet their mates.*

In 1987 Fender ventured south of the border to establish a plant in Ensenada, Baja California, Mexico. The new facility provided a considerable savings in labor costs, while still allowing for easy control of quality and production from Fender's main factory 180 miles north in Corona. Moreover, the launch of Mexican-made Fenders helped slot more affordable lines of genuine North American–made Fender guitars and amps in between the Asian-made Squiers and US-made Fenders, providing broad coverage of the market.

Fender amplifiers began rolling out of Mexico in 1989, and guitars joined in 1991. Production numbers of around 175 instruments a day in 1992 ramped up to 600 a day by 1995—following the rebuilding of the factory after a fire in

1994. By 1998 the Ensenada facility boasted a workforce approximately forty percent larger than that of the main facility in Corona, producing nearly twice the number of instruments.

By this time Mexican production had taken over the Standard line of Fender guitars that had been produced in Japan since the early 1980s, while the Japanese Fenders were relegated mostly to domestic sales in Japan. By 1999 the Ensenada factory was turning out several guitar lines that would experience enduring popularity. Among them were the Classic '50s, '60s, and '70s Stratocasters and the Classic '50s Telecaster, which were joined by a Classic '60s Telecaster with rosewood fingerboard in 2001.

Production further bloomed into several creatively revised and modified renditions of longtime favorites, including the Traditional Fat Strat, Deluxe Nashville Tele, Deluxe Powerhouse Strat, and the Tex-Mex Strat (later renamed the Jimmie Vaughan Tex-Mex Stratocaster), along with a pair of new offset-inspired designs: the Toronado and Cyclone.

A few years later Fender also applied a touch of the Custom Shop's Relic series to Mexican-made guitars with the popular Road Worn series, which brought that played-in look and feel at a much more affordable price range. Since then Mexican-made Fender instruments and amplifiers have continued to deliver great value in several classic and creative models.

ABOVE AND LEFT: *Jimmie Vaughan
performs at the 2008 NAMM show.*
BELOW: *Bill Schultz in front of the
rebuilt Ensenada factory in 1994.*
RIGHT: *A three-pickup Cyclone.*

New Factory for Corona and Amps Advance

BELOW: *Assembly of a '65 Deluxe Reverb Reissue.* OPPOSITE: *Michael Landau with a complement of Hot Rod amps. In 2002 Fender moved production of its core tube amps, including the Hot Rod Deluxe and DeVille, to Enseneda.*

With Mexican production helping to take up the slack, Fender built a new, state-of-the-art factory for the US in Corona, California, in 1998. Since the purchase of Fender from CBS in 1985, production had spread across ten buildings and a total of 115,000 square feet. In addition to consolidating Fender under one roof, the new $20 million, 177,000-square-foot building included several new boons to overall efficiency, allowed room for expansion, and boasted a new zero-toxic-emissions finishing department.

The latter was important for statutory compliance with California's strict environmental codes, and it also made it possible to safely spray chemical treatments like nitrocellulose lacquer, which was part of what allowed Fender to bring production of the Relic Series guitars back entirely in house.

Meanwhile, the amplifier range was expanding in several directions, via production both in Mexico and the US. The year 2001 saw a pair of offerings that represented opposite ends of the

spectrum, covering the best of Fender's tube-fired past and the first foray into the potential of digital technology to enable bold new sounds for the future: the American-made '65 Super Reverb recaptured the classic 4×10 combo from the blackface era, a favorite of blues and rock players alike, while the Mexican-made Cyber-Twin packed a powerful digital signal processor (DSP) to deliver a virtual amp collection in a box.

The following year, Fender added the smaller Cyber-Deluxe combo, while also moving production of tube amps in Fender's popular core series—including the Pro Junior, Blues Junior, Blues and

Hot Rod Deluxe, and DeVille—to the Ensenada plant. In 2003 the petite Cyber-Champ brought more compact digital capabilities to the practice-amp range while, again at the other end of the spectrum, the '64 Vibroverb Custom re-created one of the late Stevie Ray Vaughan's favorite 1×15 combos, with modifications suggested by SRV's own tech, Cesar Diaz.

And so it went, with innovations coming thick and fast, continuing to span reissue-style recognition of Fender's past tube-driven glories (sometimes in slightly modified packages) and entirely forward-looking guitar solutions lodged firmly in the twenty-first century.

Some other highlights of the 2000s and 2010s included the following:

2005–2007

- Custom Shop '57 Twin-Amp, a re-creation of the 2×12 tweed Twin favored by Eric Clapton, Keith Richards, and others

- '59 Bassman Ltd, upgrading the 4×10 reissue with improved cabinet construction and a stock 5AR4 tube rectifier

- The 1×8 G-DEC (Guitar Digital Entertainment Center) combo, a new concept in practice amps, with seventeen amplifier emulations, twenty-nine effects, and backing tracks

- Princeton Recording Amp, a re-creation of the blackface-era Princeton Reverb with space for a built-in, rack-mounted compressor, overdrive, and attenuator—in a traditional 1×10 cabinet

- The 60-watt 1×12 Super-Sonic combo blending classic Fender clean and crunch tones with high-gain lead tones in a powerful channel-switching package

- The '57 Deluxe, a long-awaited reissue of the beloved 5E3 tweed combo

- Champion 600, with the look of some of the earliest Fender amplifiers, plus a little extra gain up front

LEFT: *The G-DEC at the 2010 NAMM show Fender amp display.* OPPOSITE: *Introduced in 2019, the Tone Master series of digital modeling amps includes a Princeton Reverb, Twin Reverb, Super Reverb, and Deluxe Reverb in both black and blond (seen here).*

2011–2012

- The Mustang III combo, packing twelve digital amp models and thirty-seven effects into a 100-watt, 1×12 combo

- Two signature Eric Clapton Custom Shop combos: the 18-watt EC Tremolux and 45-watt EC Twinolux, both with bias-modulating tremolo

- The Machete, a 50-watt, two-channel head capable of both scorching high gain and crystalline cleans

- Jazz great George Benson co-designs the first signature Hot Rod model featuring a single Jensen C12K speaker and 12AT7 preamp tube

2014–2016

- The '68 Custom Princeton Reverb, paying tribute to the early silverface styling with drip-edge grille surround

- The Edge Deluxe, a hand-wired tweed 5E3 combo upgraded with the U2 guitarist's choice of a Celestion Alnico Blue speaker

- The Bassbreaker series, an homage to the tweed Bassman's rock 'n' roll roots in 7-, 15-, 30-, and 45-watt models, with hot-rodded styling

2019

- '62 Princeton-Amp Chris Stapleton Edition, a brownface combo dedicated to the Nashville-based singer, songwriter, and producer

- The Tone Master Twin Reverb and Deluxe Reverb, Chinese-made digital combos dedicated to producing one classic sound each

As Fender roars into its fourth quarter century, the sounds available from its classic tube amps of several decades ago remain as popular as ever—and just as versatile amid the maelstrom of popular music today—while the company's forward-looking attitude toward new technology continues to reshape those legendary tones into new packages to suit the needs of contemporary guitarists and bassists.

Comprehensive as it already was, by 2023 Fender's amp lineup boasted even more new models and several additions to popular existing series.

Proving an overnight success, the Tone Master digital series launched in 2019 later gained 1x10-inch Princeton Reverb and 4x10-inch Super Reverb combos, while the '68 Custom tube series expanded to five models. Joining the Artist Signature line, the ACB 50 was designed in collaboration with U2 bassist Adam Clayton and represented a creative update of the medium-sized, tube-powered bass combo that helped put Fender on the map some seventy years earlier.

ABOVE: *Pino Palladino and his mighty Super Bassman stacks with the Who.*
OPPOSITE: *Jazz great George Benson with the first signature amp in the Hot Rod line.*

Chapter

13

PRO
SHOP

Vintage Reissues and Modern Masterpieces

Fender's production and design successes during the Bill Schultz era reintroduced this company's classics to the world and added several new models that bring fresh, exciting features to the table, all while building on a solid foundation grounded in that time-tested Fender sound, look, and feel.

The American Vintage Reissue Series remained immensely popular through the 2000s and into the 2010s. A raft of new models added in 2012 represented classic Telecasters, Stratocasters and Jazzmasters from alternative years in the 1950s and 1960s, while the name of the line itself was slightly tweaked to American Vintage Series. In 2018 this entire vintage-inspired lineup was given a thoughtful overhaul, becoming the American Originals Series of guitars and basses, made to 1950s, 1960s, and 1970s specs and spanning a wider range of original models than either preceding series.

Launched back in 1987, the flagship line of contemporary models—the American Standard Series—was revamped in 2011. The new American Professional Series, as it was renamed in 2017, added a host of cutting-edge specs and features to a wide range of models that retained the most important aspects of their predecessors in visuals, sonics, and overall vibe, delivering a lineup of new guitars that were still entirely Fender, but suited to the broader vocabulary that today's guitarist often requires.

Fender | AMERICAN PROFESSIONAL
Corona, Ca

Not to be left out of the makeover, the more affordable Fenders from the Ensenada plant in Mexico were restyled as the Vintera Series. In addition to ably living up to its premise of capturing "*Vint*age style for the modern *era*," this line delivered a striking number of new and interesting models in a wide range of options—a whopping nineteen variations of eight guitars and basses (*not* including various finish and neck-shape options), including fun new arrivals such as an early-1960s-style Telecaster with Bigsby, an early-1970s Telecaster Custom with neck humbucker and four control knobs, a 1960s Mustang Bass, a 1960s Jaguar in both original format and Modified HH (dual humbuckers), and 1950s and 1960s Stratocasters with both vintage and Modified features.

Creative Contemporaries

As the late 2010s rolled toward our current decade, FMIC offered many inspired offerings, including several new models and lines that further embraced the marriage of vintage and modern without taking matters too far beyond what players expect from a classic Fender guitar or bass.

Neither a model nor a line as such, one new program sparked the interest of players looking for a bespoke variation on a new model without investing in Custom Shop pricing. Launched in 2016, the Mod Shop employed what Fender called "an immersive digital studio experience," enabling customers to design the look, feel, and sound of their guitar and bass, to be built at the Corona factory and ready for delivery in thirty days. Initially the Mod Shop had the Telecaster, Stratocaster, Precision Bass, and Jazz Bass available for ordering, later adding the Acoustasonic and Jazzmaster, all with myriad options for finish colors, pickguard materials, neck and fingerboard configurations, pickups, bridges, tuners, and other design aspects.

Taking an artful stab at the what-if? school of electric-guitar design, Fender launched its Parallel Universe series in 2018. The premise: what if classic-era Fender models swapped and shared several components and design features to produce a range of Fender classics that might have been? The results have included an ongoing series of exciting new guitars that look, feel, and sound entirely Fender, but that combine elements never before included on the same model. Among others, the Sixty-Six (an HSS Strat-like guitar with a compacted Jazz Bass body and other original features), the Meteora (a space-aged offset design with Tele electronics in Edition One and dual humbuckers in Edition Two), and the Maverick Dorado (a six-string with Maverick body shape, Electric XII–style neck with hockey-stick headstock, and two Tim Shaw Filter'Tron-style humbuckers) have delivered fun "classic Fenders that never were," all while enabling entirely new tones and visuals.

OPPOSITE TOP LEFT: *George Blanda measures an early '50s Telecaster to update the American Vintage Series.*
OPPOSITE TOP RIGHT: *An American Vintage 1964 Telecaster and "case candy."*
OPPOSITE BOTTOM LEFT: *Fender's Dave Wronksi files nut slots on an American Professional Telecaster.*
OPPOSITE BOTTOM RIGHT: *An American Vintage Jaguar.*
BELOW: *A Player Plus Meteora in Silverburst with its dual Fireball humbucking pickups.*

Pedal Redux and a Tele Hybrid

Also in 2018, Fender returned to the effects pedal market, a sector that it hadn't addressed since a line of the late 1960s and 1970s that included the cult-favorite Fender Blender octave-fuzz unit. Using original circuits designed in-house, this extensive range has blossomed to twenty-three high-quality effects pedals, all built in custom-grade, folded-metal enclosures with the iconic Fender amp-style jewel pilot lights. Several employ multiple footswitches to access a variety of features, and three MTG pedals carry actual vacuum tubes. One of these, the MTG Tube Tremolo, was designed by noted amp maker Bruce Egnater.

In late 2022 Fender released a more affordable line of compact effects pedals in the Hammertone Series. Finished in a durable Hammerite-style enamel and wearing the iconic "witch-hat" knobs used on the semi-hollow Starcaster guitar of the '70s, the full Hammertone range included the eponymously named Overdrive, Distortion, Fuzz, Metal, Reverb, Delay, Space Delay, Flanger, and Chorus.

RIGHT: *Released in 2022, the eponymously named Hammertone line of effects pedals features a classic Hammerite finish and "witch hat" knobs.*
OPPOSITE: *The American Acoustasonic Telecaster released in 2019 has since been joined by the Acoustasonic Stratocaster and Acoustasonic Jazzmaster.*

The American Acoustasonic Telecaster, released early in 2019, achieved both industry buzz and player interest matched by very few hybrid electric-acoustic guitars of the past from any manufacturer. It has since been joined by the American Acoustasonic Stratocaster and Acoustasonic Jazzmaster, plus the more streamlined and more affordable Player Telecaster and Player Jazzmaster. Patterns on fully hollow bodies made these iconic Fender shapes, with solid spruce tops and mahogany back and sides, the American Acoustasonic models sport a noiseless Tele-style magnetic pickup in

the bridge position, a Fishman under-saddle transducer, and a Fender-Fishman codesigned Acoustic Engine to blend the two into any of ten available acoustic body shapes and styles. The result is a series of superbly versatile instruments in relatively compact, comfortable packages that both belie their capabilities while presenting forms familiar to players more accustomed to the electric format.

American Ultras and Artists Abound

Toward the latter part of 2019, Fender introduced the American Ultra series, a new Corona-made flagship lineup of guitars and basses that applied the best cutting-edge features and designs to the traditional styling of classic Fenders. As Fender VP Max Gutnik put it at the time, "Ultra is a great example of the continued evolution of Fender's classic instruments in a way that remains true to Fender's original creation yet advances the instrument to serve modern players of all genres."[62] The full series includes several variations on the Stratocaster, Jazzmaster, and Telecaster, plus the Precision Bass, Jazz Bass, and Jazz Bass V. Extending a similar brief to more affordable guitars made at Fender's Ensenada facility, the Player Plus series arrived in 2021 with a bevy of familiar shapes loaded with twenty-first century features, such as noiseless pickups, contemporary hardware, and modern neck shapes.

In 2020 the popular American Professional series was updated after just three years into the American Professional II. Designed to sit better as the sweet spot between several others in the American-made lineup, this series features variations on the most popular guitar and bass models, with looks and vibes that appeal to vintage-leaning players, plus features that subtly update the format to the needs of today's guitarists.

THIS PAGE: In 2020 the popular American Professional series was updated into the American Professional II. OPPOSITE TOP: Eric Burton of the Black Pumas. OPPOSITE BOTTOM LEFT: Tom Morello and his Soul Power Stratocaster. OPPOSITE BOTTOM RIGHT: Notable among some of the more recent Artist releases is the Jason Isbell Custom Telecaster.

Then, early in 2020, Fender launched its ambitious Stories Collection with the Eric Johnson "Virginia" Stratocaster, a guitar designed to capture the vintage look of Johnson's former prized 1954 Stratocaster—a rare early Strat made with sassafras wood rather than ash—with a few artist-introduced modifications. "When I got the prototype from Fender," Johnson commented, "it had the tone I had been looking for since my original guitar. It has a particularly smooth, sustained tone, but as you turn it up it has gain like a little violin."[63]

Projects like the Stories Collection were born out of the intention to reproduce specific legendary artists' guitars that have particularly trenchant stories to tell, either constructed in a Limited Edition by the Custom Shop or, for one year of production, at the Corona factory. Following Eric Johnson's "Virginia," Fender applied the dual-production process to re-creations of studio ace Brent Mason's Telecasters—one of the most recorded guitars in history—and others are reported to be in the works.

Toward the other end of the spectrum, other recent Artist models included a "Soul Power" Stratocaster for Tom Morello, a Jazzmaster for Jim Root of aggressive metal merchants Slipknot, and a Deluxe Precision Bass for Duff McKagan.

Fender also closed out its seventy-fourth year in a big way, prior to the anniversary in 2021, with new Artist Signature models for Jimmy Page, Jimi Hendrix, and the R&B star H.E.R., who busted out a preview of the model at the 2019 Grammy Awards—a clear acrylic Stratocaster made by Custom Shop master builder Scott Buehl—to wail on for the closing solo to her song "Anti."

Fender has had a long list of productive collaborations with artists over the years, a trend in Signature models that largely began with the Custom Shop but spread throughout the lines over the past couple of decades. Through the company's seventy-fifth anniversary and beyond, a plethora of Artist models have remained among Fender's most popular, and most interesting, offerings.

Fifty guitars strong as of 2023 (*excluding* the Custom Shop offerings), the Artist series of guitars made in Corona and Ensenada continue to do what Fender has often done best in the past two decades: present a varied lineup of extremely popular models that capture a range of both vintage and modern specs, along with the specific needs and design points of the stars who have made them iconic. Notable among some of the more recent Artist releases are the Troy Van Leeuwen Jazzmaster, Johnny Marr Jaguar, Cory Wong Stratocaster, Ben Gibbard Mustang, Jason Isbell Custom Telecaster, and other desirable offerings. As ever, in addition to appealing to fans of the artists, the guitars themselves offer interesting and original sets of specifications that players might not find in other models, regardless of fandom.

In another fun twist in 2023, Fender launched the Gold Foil series. Initially including two colorways each for the Jazzmaster, Stratocaster, and Jazz Bass, the line takes the unusual step of using solid mahogany bodies on the guitars (alder on the basses) and equips them with recreations of the '60s catalog-guitar pickups that have become extremely popular in the 2010s and '20s. The results are heard in several enticing new tones from guitars and basses sporting the familiar Fender playability and construction quality.

LEFT: *John 5 at the Fender factory with his signature double-neck.* **OPPOSITE TOP:** *Duff McKagan with his signature bass.* **OPPOSITE BOTTOM:** *Brent Mason and his Signature Telecaster.*

FUTURE
PERFECT

Looking Ahead

As Fender enters the third decade of the twenty-first century to begin its next seventy-five years, it does so with all the advantages of a company at the forefront of the postmodern age of the electric guitar. Players have long embraced the instrument's modernity—the upgrades, improvements, and bonus features—yet Fender's guitar, bass, and amplifier classics from the first couple decades of its existence remain entirely relevant, and highly desirable, when reproduced in as close to their original vintage forms as possible today.

It can be easy to overlook the fact that Fender's continued success is a testament to the people who have carried Leo Fender's and Don Randall's visions from the middle of the last century to well into the twenty-first century. Several hard-working heroes of the latter-day company deserve recognition. Richard McDonald became head of marketing at Fender during the formative Bill Schultz era and retired in 2019 as chief product strategist after winning the Music & Sound Retailer's Lifetime Achievement/ Hall of Fame award at the 2018 winter NAMM show. McDonald's leadership helped form the foundation for Fender's current success, and his commitment to creating not just guitars but *guitar players* is a vision that resonates in FMIC's digital products—both hardware and application software.

Fender has continued to grow by embracing the full spectrum of vintage-to-modern, a progression embodied in the American Original, American Professional, and American Ultra guitar series (with the more affordable Vinteras falling somewhere between the first two of these). But what does that leave the company to work toward for the future? Does Fender's current broad coverage leave nowhere to go but the tech-loaded products that seek to rival other compact consumer electronics?

According to Fender CEO Andy Mooney, players shouldn't hold their breath awaiting the eStrat, iMaster, or some other breed of ephemeral instrument chasing a trend that has already largely passed by the time it hits the market.

"Guitar players have rejected technology embedded within guitars for years," says Mooney, "as the technologies employed didn't solve a problem and were often poorly executed. The only exception I'm aware of is the success of our own American Acoustasonic Series, which utilizes sonic modeling technology developed in collaboration with Fishman Electronics."[64]

What that leaves for Fender in the future, then, is the advantage of playing from a position of comfort: leaning on the acknowledged strengths the brand has built by recognizing so much of what was right with classic Fender designs in the first place and continuing to follow the vision of the company's founder.

MAIN:
The Acoustasonic Stratocaster.

RIGHT:
Richard McDonald became head of marketing at Fender during the formative Bill Schultz era, and his leadership helped form a foundation for Fender's current success. McDonald retired in 2019.

"Leo Fender's designs are timeless because his design philosophy was that 'form must follow function,'" Mooney confirms. "He solved problems working musicians had in the '50s and '60s, and still have now. Leo believed that 'artists were angels and his job was to give them wings to fly.' This has become Fender's Vision Statement and continues to guide everything we do."

If this meant primarily selling to a relatively narrow, professional clientele in the early days of the company, however, Fender's reach has broadened immeasurably in the years since.

As Mooney puts it "Fender's focus for decades was solely on serving the needs of working musicians, many of them highly accomplished. Today we're equally focused on serving the needs of first-time players with products and services like Fender Play. Today we not only strive to give future artists the wings to fly, we strive to teach them *how* to fly."

Whatever the coming decades might bring, it's difficult to imagine popular music being made without Fender instruments and amplifiers, old and new alike, continuing to shape and inspire the soundtracks to our lives.

OPPOSITE: *Fender CEO Andy Mooney on stage with a Telecaster Deluxe.*
MAIN: *Fender Play takes the needs of student players into the future.*
INSET: *Addressing the student market, six decades past.*

References

1. Richard Smith, *Fender: The Sound Heard 'Round the World*, p. 7 (Hal Leonard, 2003).

2. Interview with Leo Fender, *Guitar Player*, 1971.

3. Ibid.

4. John Teagle & John Sprung, *Fender Amps: The First 50 Years*, p. 59 (Hal Leonard, 1995).

5. Interview with Leo Fender, *Guitar Player*, May 1978.

6. George Fullerton interview by Tony Bacon conducted in the early 1990s for *The Fender Book*, published on Reverb.com February 8, 2018.

7. Leo Fender talking to Forrest White, as recounted in *Fender: The Inside Story*, p. 15 (Miller Freeman Books, 1994).

8. Ibid, pp. 17–18.

9. Andy Volk, *Lap Steel Guitar* (Centerstream Publications, 2003).

10. Detlef Schmidt, *Fender Precision Basses: 1951–1954*, p. 109 (Centerstream Publishing, 2010).

11. Leo Fender interview, *Guitar Player*, 1978.

12. Leo Fender interview, *Rolling Stone*, 1976.

13. Forrest White, *Fender: The Inside Story*, p. 44 (Miller Freeman Books, 1994).

14. Tony Bacon, 1992 interview with Don Randall, published November 1, 2018, on Reverb.com as "Fender's Don Randall Offers Revisionist Take on Leo, CBS, and the Company's Early Days/Bacon's Archive."

15. Ibid.

16. Forrest White, *Fender: The Inside Story*, p. 41 (Miller Freeman Books, 1994).

17. Leo Fender interviewed in *Guitar Player*, 1984.

18. Ibid.

19. George Fullerton interview by Tony Bacon conducted in the early 1990s for *The Fender Book*, published on Reverb.com February 8, 2018.

20. George Gruhn and Walter Carter, *Gruhn's Guide to Vintage Guitars* (Backbeat Books, revised 2010).

21. Tony Bacon and Barry Moorhouse, *The Bass Book*, p. 9 (GPI Books, 1995).

22. Ibid, p. 10.

23. George Fullerton interview by Tony Bacon conducted in the early 1990s for *The Fender Book*, published on Reverb.com February 8, 2018.

24. George Fullerton interview by Tony Bacon conducted in the early 1990s for *The Fender Book*, published on Reverb.com, February 8, 2018.

25. A. R. Duchossoir, *The Fender Stratocaster*, p. 9 (Hal Leonard, 1994).

26. Tom Wheeler, *The Stratocaster Chronicles*, p. 62 (Hal Leonard, 2004).

27. Shanon Wianecki, *Hanahou*, September 2012.

28. A. R. Duchossoir, *The Fender Stratocaster*, p. 7 (Hal Leonard, 1994).

29. Richard Smith, *Fender: The Sound Heard 'Round the World* (Hal Leonard, 2010).

30. George Fullerton interview by Tony Bacon conducted in the early 1990s for *The Fender Book*, published on Reverb.com Feb 8, 2018.

31. Bill Carson interviewed by Tony Bacon conducted 1992 for *The Fender Book*, published on Reverb.com, October 3, 2019.

32. Tom Wheeler, *The Stratocaster Chronicles*, p. 50 (Hal Leonard, 2004).

33. Tony Bacon, 1992 interview with Don Randall, published November 1, 2018, on Reverb.com as "Fender's Don Randall Offers Revisionist Take on Leo, CBS, and the Company's Early Days/Bacon's Archive."

34. Tom Wheeler, *The Soul of Tone: Celebrating 60 Years of Fender Amps*, p. 177 (Hal Leonard, 2007).

35. Don Randall, NAMM Oral Histories interview, 2006.

36. Tom Wheeler, *The Soul of Tone: Celebrating 60 Years of Fender Amps*, p. 177 (Hal Leonard, 2007).

37. Ibid, p. 164.

38. Robert Perine, "How I Helped Leo Fender," *Vintage Guitar*, May 2003.

39. Ibid.

40. A. R. Duchossoir, *The Fender Stratocaster*, p. 17 (Hal Leonard, 1994).

41. Interview with Chris Fleming, Dave Hunter, *The Electric Guitar Sourcebook*, p. 184 (Backbeat Books, 2006).

42. Forrest White, *Fender: The Inside Story*, p. 146 (Miller Freeman Books, 1994).

43. Interview with Leo Fender, *Guitar Player*, September 1971.

44. Interview with Leo Fender, *Guitar Player*, September 1971.

45. Addison Nugent, "The Day Herbie Hancock Met the Electric Piano," OZY.com.

46. Tony Bacon, 1992 interview with Don Randall, published November 1, 2018, on Reverb.com as "Fender's Don Randall Offers Revisionist Take on Leo, CBS, and the Company's Early Days/Bacon's Archive."

47. Don Randall interview, NAMM Oral Histories video series, 2006.

48. John Page interview, conducted by Dave Hunter, October 2019.

49. Tony Bacon and Paul Day, *The Fender Book*, p. 58 (Balafon Books, 1998).

50. Bill Schultz, NAMM Oral Histories interview, March 2003.

51. John Page interview, conducted by Dave Hunter, October 2019.

52. Bill Schultz, NAMM Oral Histories interview, March 2003.

53. Michael Stevens interview, conducted by Dave Hunter, September 2017.

54. John Page interview, conducted by Dave Hunter, September 2017.

55. Ibid.

56. Michael Stevens interview, conducted by Dave Hunter, September 2017.

57. John Page interview, conducted by Dave Hunter, September 2017.

58. J. Black interview, conducted by Dave Hunter, September 2017.

59. Ibid.

60. Vince Cunetto interview, conducted by Dave Hunter, September 2017.

61. Ron Thorn interview, conducted by Dave Hunter, March 2019.

62. VP Max Gutnik, Fender.com, January 2020.

63. Eric Johnson, Fender.com, February 2020.

64. Interview with Fender CEO Andy Mooney, Dave Hunter, July 2020 (and all attributed quotes after).

Image Credits

Author Bio

Acknowledgments

Dave Hunter is a writer and musician who has worked extensively in the UK and the US. He is the author of *The Fender Telecaster, The Fender Stratocaster, The Gibson Les Paul, Star Guitars, The Guitar Amp Handbook, Guitar Effects Pedals, The British Amp Invasion, The Guitar Pickup Handbook,* and several other titles. Hunter is also a regular contributor to *Guitar Player, Vintage Guitar,* and *Premier Guitar* magazines in the US, and *Guitar Magazine* in the UK, and is a contributing essayist to the United States Library of Congress National Recording Preservation Board's Permanent Archive. He lives in Portsmouth, New Hampshire, with his wife and their two children.

I would like to thank Rich Siegle (whose photo research was key to this project), Najla Quarry, Dan Heitkemper, Christina Stejskal, Heather Youmans, and Justin Norvell at Fender, all of whom were enormously helpful in providing information and archival images, and John Page, Michael Stevens, Chris Fleming, Vince Cunetto, Ron Thorn, and Andy Mooney of Fender past and present for agreeing to be interviewed. Many thanks to Matthew Logan Vasquez for relaying questions to his grandmother, Irene Vasquez. Thanks to Bruce Derr for enthusiastically sharing his knowledge of the early Fender steel players, and to David and Paige Davidson and Maddie Patch at Well Strung Guitars for photographic access to their stock of vintage Fender guitars and all the hard work in sorting and sending, as well as the long list of owners and photographers (named individually in our photo credits) who contributed images to this book.

A heartfelt thanks to my editor Dennis Pernu, as well as Steve Roth, Jessi Schatz, Regina Grenier, Barbara States, Brooke Pelletier, and Zack Miller at Quarto/Motorbooks for all their efforts in helping this project fly, and to Tom Lewis for the attentive copy editing. Thanks, too, to authors Tony Bacon, Tom Wheeler, and Richard Smith for laying so much invaluable groundwork in this field in the form of original interviews with personnel who are no longer with us from the early days of Fender. Thanks, as always, to my wife Jess and our children Fred and Flo, and a sincere thanks, finally, to that guy who advertised his stripped and refinished 1965 Duo-Sonic II in the classified ads of the *Cincinnati Enquirer* all those years ago, which, at the princely sum of $100, became my first Fender electric guitar.

Index

First Published in 2021. Second Edition Published in 2023
by Motorbooks, an imprint of The Quarto Group,
100 Cummings Center, Suite 265-D, Beverly, MA 01915, USA.
T (978) 282-9590 F (978) 283-2742

Motorbooks titles are also available at discount for retail, wholesale, promotional,
and bulk purchase. For details, contact the Special Sales Manager by email at
specialsales@quarto.com or by mail at The Quarto Group, Attn: Special Sales
Manager, 100 Cummings Center, Suite 265-D, Beverly, MA 01915, USA.

27 26 25 24 23   1 2 3 4 5 6

ISBN: 978-0-7603-8730-6

Digital edition published in 2023
eISBN: 978-0-7603-8731-3

Library of Congress Cataloging-in-Publication Data Available

Acquiring Editor: Dennis Pernu
Design: Traffic
Layout: Cindy Samargia Laun

Printed in China